Dance
of Stones

A Shamanic Road Trip

To John
mary all your
road trips be shamanic!

Kenn Day

Dance
of Stones

A Shamanic Road Trip

Kenn Day

MOON
BOOKS

Winchester, UK
Washington, USA

First published by Moon Books, 2013
Moon Books is an imprint of John Hunt Publishing Ltd., Laurel House, Station Approach,
Alresford, Hants, SO24 9JH, UK
office1@jhpbooks.net
www.johnhuntpublishing.com
www.moon-books.net

For distributor details and how to order please visit the 'Ordering' section on our website.

Text copyright: Kenn Day 2013

ISBN: 978 1 78279 308 3

A CIP catalogue record for this book is available from the British Library.

Printed in the USA by Edwards Brothers Malloy

We operate a distinctive and ethical publishing philosophy in all
areas of our business, from our global network of authors to
production and worldwide distribution.

Dedication

This work is dedicated to my ancestors of blood and spirit
— to all of those upon whose shoulders I stand.

Acknowledgments

Many people have assisted in the process of writing this book. I would like to thank "Soli" and her family, without which this would have been a very different, and less interesting, book. I had two editors at different times during the process. My thanks to both Linda and Heather for their work. I have a great deal of gratitude to my shamanic students, apprentices and others who read the manuscript at various stages and offered their feedback, especially Candace, Lynn, Mar and Renea. Finally, I offer my deepest gratitude, appreciation and love to my greatest resource, my wife Patricia. Her refusal to allow me to accept anything less than my best work has made this book the success that it is.

Table of Contents

Forward to the Second Edition

Much has changed, in the world and for me personally, since the first release of this book in 2008. The biggest change for me is that I've become a father, and am now initiated into one of the great and universal Mysteries of the human experience. The nature of Mystery is such that we cannot adequately describe them in words, and yet it is immediately apparent when one encounter a fellow initiate. This is true with parenting, as well as with trauma and shamanic initiation. I have often had the experience of meeting someone who uses the title of shaman, only to discover immediately that they have a very different definition of the term than I do. On the other hand, I have also met quite a few who definitely share that experience, whether they choose to call themselves shaman or not.

Post-Tribal Shamanism is a living tradition. It has also continued to change during the time between these two printings. While the teachings remain the same, I am gradually deepening my reception and understanding of them. In addition, my ability to express and convey the teachings is gradually improving, with the help of my teachers, students and all the other people in my life. None of the changes are reflected in the text. All I have done is correct a few typographic errors from the first printing.

I would like to express my gratitude to the fine people at John Hunt Publishing and Moon Books for making it possible to pass these teachings along.

namaste,

Kenn Day

Introduction

In traditional societies there is an accepting community to welcome the shaman into their work. The people the shaman work with in these cultures already know and accept the importance of spirits, ancestors, energy, soul and all the other things that tie humans to our world.

This is not true of the budding shamanic practitioner in the West. In many cases, a person undergoing early shamanic initiations would be considered insane by the standards of our medical establishment. The path to recognizing, accepting and working with the larger perspective of the shaman is considerably more difficult for those of us brought up in the post–tribal modern world.

Even being born into the modern Western culture today is a recipe for deep wounding. We are bereft of a huge part of the real world, along with any deep connection with ancestors or other spirits. Fortunately, we live in a world that can change. We can move from a world without spirits to a world where soul and science co–exist.

I remember learning how the world can change as a child. Reading about the British empire in school, I found that I was immediately attracted to all things English. This persisted for some years and I came to live in a world in which the British empire was obviously a Good Thing. It wasn't until many years later that I looked more deeply into the dark side of the empire, and discovered the various cruelties, betrayals and arrogance of the British. With this realization, my world changed. I no longer lived in a world in which the English were always the good guys. It may sound simplistic, but this was a profound shift for me. More importantly, it also helped me to understand how different people can live in such different worlds side–by–side.

From a shamanic perspective, the world we perceive IS the world we live in, thus it is real—even if only to us. The role of the shaman is often to assist others in the process of transforming the world they live in, and ultimately to come to the understanding that the many worlds are one world.

I hope that this book will offer an opportunity for the reader to enter a larger world. It is a story of a modern day shaman on a journey of exploration and initiation. It could easily be the story of anyone who seeks a deeper awareness of the world we live in and our own experience as human beings. In the interest of making this experience as accessible as possible, I have avoided the academic tone and footnotes of many of the books on shamanism currently available.

During the process of editing the manuscript, I had one reader who told me that she felt completely caught up in the story—felt like it was happening to her—and that Soli's experiences became hers as well. She said that she finished the book feeling that she had made the journey and been transformed by it. I can't think of a better way to read this book. If at all possible, allow it to become your own story.

At the end of many of the chapters are what I've called Deepenings. These are opportunities to go into some of what is covered in that chapter in a bit more depth. Take advantage of the exercises that are offered in some of these Deepenings and you may find that this is your journey too.

Essentially, it is my hope that you – the reader – will realize that all human beings have access to the experiences and perceptions of the shaman. It is through these that I hope we will come to recognize and revitalize our deep relationship with the world of spirit and the Mysteries of this existence.

Welcome aboard!

should and both Christine and I went out looking for her. Her nanny told us she was in the wadi behind the village, playing. I went looking there and found her building a small house—like one of the native houses—from sticks and mud. She was talking away in the native dialect—to this Neenah of course. But there was no one there!"

"It was only after I had brought her home that she told me that Neenah was really a little blue rabbit—apparently a nature spirit of some sort that had become displaced when the villagers built some new houses above the wadi. This blue rabbit apparently had persuaded her to make a house for it as well—ah! She told us quite a lot about Neenah once I got her back to the house. Apparently it helped her find lost objects and told her secrets about the other children—which naturally frightened away all of her more human companions."

Detlev pauses, as if considering this for the first time. "That was all rather uncanny—all the things it seemed she did that scared off the other children. But for some reason the little blue creature did not seem to travel well. When we moved to Stuttgart shortly after that, Neenah was not heard from again." Detlev finishes his story with a flourish like a stage magician. He obviously finds the whole thing quite amusing. I glance up at Soli leaning in the doorway behind him. Just as obviously, she finds the story anything but funny.

Deepening

Where does the shaman come from? There are quite a few answers to this deceptively simple question. We can talk about the historical source of what we call shamanism today. We can look at the various initiatory practices of indigenous people. However, perhaps the most important answer is that the shaman comes when and where he or she is called, emerging in response to the need for a shaman. This is true in many ways, on many levels. When you have an illness of the spirit or soul, there is a deep part of you that will reach out instinctively to any resource it can find. Our soul instinctively recognizes a shaman as one who can work with these deep wounds of the spirit, to bring us to wholeness.

When your soul is in pain, it may reach out unconsciously, leading you into a place where the pain can be addressed. I have had many clients come to me for something simple and purely physical—like tennis elbow—only to find that, once the tennis elbow is repaired, the real wound arises and can then be addressed.

It's important to point out at the beginning that very few are actually called to this shamanic work. Most people are blessed with other, more ordinary, talents.

But what are the needs that call to a shaman, these wounds of the soul? The need for connection; the need to know where we belong; the need to know where we come from; the need to feel that we are a part of something larger than ourselves; the need of all the parts to realize themselves as one complete whole. These are the needs we all have as human beings. When these needs are not met, we loose something of our humanity and our soul naturally seeks to reconnect with that wholeness. The shaman is one who helps us to rediscover the healing power of this deep connection.

alien to me and I feel like I've been dropped down a rabbit hole into Alice's Wonderland or something." I fasten my seat belt and take a long pull from the freshly opened water bottle.

"Is it anything like taking a shamanic journey for the first time?" Soli asks with a smile as she pulls the red Mercedes station wagon back onto the road.

I nod. "That's exactly what it feels like. You're walking around in a place that should be familiar but isn't, where you can't quite grasp the language yet, and you don't feel quite...real."

Soli is quiet for almost a minute before replying. "Then, for you, to take someone else on a shamanic journey is something like me walking through the market with you. I know the language. I've visited here before, and nothing is as unfamiliar to me. I don't get that alien feeling from it that you do."

"Yes. Except that I'm not sure I'll ever be as familiar with the shamanic worlds as you are with French markets."

"I'd like you to take me on one of your journeys with you." Soli says. I point wordlessly to our upcoming exit and she steers us smoothly around the tight spiral curve and onto the straight motorway toward Brittany. "But first I want to know more about it. I want to know more about how you become a shaman."

"That's right...ask all the easy questions up front," I quip.

"But I mean it!" she persists.

"I know you do. I'm just stalling because I don't want to recite the canned definition for you. That would be the opposite of shamanic."

Taking a deep and noisy breath, I continue. "One answer is that it's a very long path in which life teaches you how to serve as a shaman by putting you through all sorts of traumatic, challenging and life-threatening experiences. Assuming you survive, by the time that's over, you'll know your own healing process deeply enough to share it with others."

Soli frowns over the wheel. "You said 'one answer.' I certainly hope there are others as well. Perhaps even a less traumatic one that will make more sense to me?"

I want to answer from my heart, as Grandfather, my closest spiritual guide, is always reminding me to do. He consistently harps on how important it is to stay in the moment and speak truth, but it gets me in trouble more often than not, particularly when it involves relationships—whether they're with spirits or people. At the moment, my heart is feeling pretty cloudy, far away from home, so I let the answer come from my head instead. "A shaman needs to be able to act effectively, to offer information and guidance, and healing that you can't get from ordinary places. In order to do that, a shaman has to be able to create and maintain sacred space...."

"And just what is sacred space?"

So much for the condensed version.

"Do you mean like in a church?"she continues.

I let her question sink in, seeing if anything brilliant rises to the surface in response. "You remember when we were at Mystery School at that first session, and we were being led on what they called a shamanic journey?"

tribe's people, the ancestors who have died but who still maintain the identity they wore in their human life.

The upper world holds more celestial spirits, including those ancestor spirits who have come to a realization of 'Self' behind the identity they wore in human life. These spirits are ready to either move back down into the middle world, taking on a new body and name, or they may prefer to remain in the upper world, providing their descendants with spiritual guidance.

The middle world is the one we're most familiar with; it's a reflection of our own experience of daily life. For aboriginal tribes living in wilderness areas, for instance, this world is populated by the spirits of that surrounding world; the animals, trees, rocks and caves that they experience in their physical bodies have a presence in this middle world.

Each of these worlds obviously contains much more than the spirits and bodies of human beings. Universal shamanic experience suggests that the underworld tends to hold larger, deeper, and more profound manifestations than the middle world of form, while the upper world holds more ethereal and abstract complexes. For example, the underworld often holds the deepest essence of an animal species. I like to use the example of the squirrel. While there may be 20 billion squirrels in the middle world they would all be connected to the one soul of "Squirrel" (Squirrel with a capital "S") that exists in the underworld.

Unlike the underworld, the upper world manifests as lighter, higher vibrations and more ethereal energy that can even appear as abstract shapes in colorful and complex geometric forms, perhaps because it is not as bound by the physical limitations of our middle world. However, there are many who find their spirit guides or teachers in this upper world, and that teacher may look like nothing more extraordinary than an old man with a walking stick.

There is a story about the natives that first encountered the ships of the European explorers in the Americas. It is said that these natives could not see the ships that approached their shores. They saw only huge white birds skimming the water. It was only their shaman who could see what was there, perhaps because he was more used to seeing beyond his expectations of what was real. The alternative realities of books, television, movies, and computer games have prepared our brains for recognition of new and unusual shapes and concepts. This expands our ability to see what is there, and yet we still see what we are conditioned to see. There is no "old man with a walking stick", but this is how our mind makes sense of what it is experiencing, so it is a truth of a different sort.

This all leads us to yet another definition of shaman—as one who is not bound by the mundane but travels in all these three worlds. Further, it is the ability to see these other worlds overlapping the everyday experience of the middle world that allows shamans to see what we call omens.

Chapter 3
The Call of the Shaman

It is mid afternoon and we have stopped in the village of Cambrai for tea and some time out of the car. We are at the Café Pélican, at the edge of an open square paved with cobblestones, sitting in wrought iron chairs at a glass-topped iron table. All very, very French. As the waiter leaves with our order, Soli checks her "handy" for messages. "I don't know how I managed before cell phones," she exclaims. "The new communication technology is fantastic! I could almost run my office from here—if I wasn't on holiday, of course."

With this last comment, she glances over at me and her tone changes.

I say nothing, just smiling back at her, but I suspect that she is used to people complaining about her being a workaholic. Still, she seems miffed to see that there are no new messages. She puts her phone back in her purse and takes out the paperback she's been reading at every opportunity.

I'm trying to write in my travel journal, but can't get beyond a description of the square, and its lazy pigeons who can't be bothered to run after scraps of food strewn across the stones. Instead, they waddle gracelessly toward them in hordes of dun and grey, as if from habit rather than hunger. My mind is pleasantly numb. I am wondering if the coffee I ordered will be as good as I imagine it to be from the dark-edged aroma drifting from nearby tables. A faint breeze rises and I tilt my face up to catch it and feel the warm sun soak my skin. Though I am feeling rather deliciously lazy myself at the moment, Soli's energy is throbbing like a silent alarm and it bothers me a bit that we are not on the same page. I wonder for a moment if it's even worth exploring. It's tempting to just wait until she explodes and deal with it then, but I suspect it would be better to let off some of the pressure now. Some people just need to process externally and Soli is certainly one of them. I—on the other hand—am one of those who prefer my processing in the comfort and safety of my own internal world. I smile—inwardly, of course—and open myself up a little more toward Soli. The sun will be as warm and lazy, even if I do exert myself a bit.

"What is so fascinating about that book?" I ask her.

Soli seems to appreciate the interruption. "I'm always looking for stories about powerful women," she replies. "I want to make my work count for something besides a paycheck, and producing films that empower women—and others, of course—is very important to me." She sets the book on the table, opened face down. "The problem is finding good writers to turn the stories I find into workable scripts."

"You have the ideas—why not write the scripts yourself?"

Soli brushes the thought way. "Not me. My writing is shit." With that she snatches the book back up and leaves me to my own devices—perhaps she is not quite so interested in processing externally as I had thought.

Looking around for something to entertain me now that I've stirred myself out of my lethargy, I notice a family sitting at the table behind Soli. A solid, red-faced father with bright blonde hair and a tight collar sits with his more refined wife and their two young children. I feel heavy and uncomfortable just looking at them, and I find myself thinking "a typical German family". Where did that come from, I wonder, then I tune into their voices and realize that they have been speaking German. I just wasn't paying attention. As I focus in more closely, trying to eavesdrop without being overly nosey, I extend my medicine body and sort of "taste" their energy, only to draw back quickly from the bitter, metallic note that vibrates through me—like fingernails on a chalkboard.

Though the couple are obviously trying to keep their voices down, the biting edge to their words—and their almost explosively angry energy—reveals that they are on the verge of having a full blown, teutonic argument. Perhaps sensing their tension, the youngest of the two boys slides out of his chair and is soon peering at me from under the table. His expression is blank at first, not realizing that I see him. But when I wink at him, he slowly returns my grin— instinctively knowing that we share a secret escape from the absurdities of angry parents, long car rides and mobile phones.

My German is just adequate to make out that they are discussing someone she knows—a male someone. Ah! That's it. He is getting married and they are here in Cambrai to attend this someone's wedding. It is clear that he is an old friend of the wife's—not the husband's. Apparently he has rented a chateau at which they are invited to stay for the weekend. The husband is arguing rather forcefully that they should take a room in town: that he told her to book them a room at the hotel and that she has forgotten on purpose so that they will have to stay with…her friend.

Soli stops reading and glances up at me. She seems to intuit that I am listening to the people behind her and I watch her eyes as she tunes into the conversation herself. After a few moments, she begins to grimace and shake her head. Leaning across the table, I try to find out if she has picked up anything more than I can with my limited German.

She leans toward me and whispers, "Well! They are here for the wedding of an old school chum. Apparently there was something between this fellow who's getting married and the woman here, because she really wants to stay at the chateau and her husband really wants to get out of there as soon as the ceremony is over and stay somewhere else. Neither one is really talking about what's getting them so angry though. It's all just little comments that make me think he's jealous. Wait..."

The older boy is grabbing his parent's attention by pointing out that his brother has snuck under the table. The father angrily snatches him out from under the table by his ear, prompting a painful squeal, picks him up under one arm and, dragging the older son along by his other arm, heads across the street toward the car park.

Soli has an evil grin on her face as she pulls her phone out of her purse and turns to the young wife: "Entschuldegung genagede frau." My German is not good enough to follow the conversation from here, but I see the woman trying to politely wave off help from Soli and her phone. I hear the car door slam as the father locks the two boys away in the flashy black BMW. Soli insists and by the time the husband returns, she is talking to another voice on the phone—something about a room for the night. She asks the couple something and he answers; she passes on the information and hangs up. He thanks her with a triumphant smile, while his wife just glares and Soli grins back entirely too innocently.

The waiter returns with our coffee, tea and croissants, then turns to give the bill to the German couple. Soli seems smugly satisfied with her interference and is moving on to more important things—like tea.

It occurs to me that this is twice now that we have run across people on the verge of an argument, and twice that Soli has interfered, in however small a way. I'm hoping that this isn't setting the tone for our whole trip together. But it does seem like there's something I need to pay attention to here.

Fishing her tea strainer out of the china cup, she meticulously shakes it dry before setting it in her spoon, then leans forward, resting her elbows on the table and says, "You know, I've been thinking more about this whole thing of becoming a shaman. Really it seems to be just a matter of learning how to put yourself into an altered state of consciousness and back again? Is that all it takes?"

"Hmm. No," I reply, holding the coffee cup with both hands and letting the rich aroma ground me more deeply into my physical senses. "That makes it sound like anyone can become a shaman just by learning how to go into a trance. And it's not quite as easy as that. The thing is, unlike becoming a lawyer, or plumber or computer programmer—"

Soli butts in with a mischievous grin, "But you said earlier that it is no different than, what? —being a plumber."

"One thing you'll notice about shamans—we're full of paradoxes." I take a sip of the coffee. It's too hot to really taste yet, but the smell is wonderfully dark and inviting. I take another sip, just to savor the intensity of it and then set the cup back in its saucer and add a good shot of milk. "What I mean to say is, that there are no courses to take or books to read that can make you a shaman. You have to be…called…to shamanize. I know that sounds weird, religious even, but that's the way it is."

Behind Soli, the father is asking the waiter for directions now, while his wife looks away. Following her gaze, I realize that she is looking into the window of the cafe. Then I see that it is the reflection she is looking at, and our eyes meet for a moment in the mirror of the window and I can feel her tension and something more beneath the surface, then she turns away. "It's a little like having a talent for something like music or art. No matter how long you go to art school, if you don't have the talent for it, you'll never really be an artist. It's like that with shamanism as well. No matter how many books you read or degrees you get, if you don't have the talent or calling to do the work, it just won't happen. Or at best, you'll make an ineffective shaman."

Soli has drawn her palm pilot out and is taking notes, tapping her stylus against her chin. "So how does one know if they are 'called' to be a shaman?"

"It all depends…it could be that you get really sick, and nothing makes you better until a shaman comes and heals you, and then you're fascinated by it from then on." I've been stirring my coffee, letting it cool, and now I take another sip—perfect! "It could be that you start having dreams or visions where you're told that you are supposed to be a shaman, and they keep up until you find some way to do it. Or maybe you get hit by lightning one day and wake up just knowing that you need to be a shaman." Pulling off a bite of my croissant, I dunk it into my coffee and pop it into my mouth for a moment of minor ecstasy. "But all that works better when you live in a part of the world where shamans, or whatever they call them in that particular neighborhood, are a part of life as you know it. Not something strange at all. I think in this part of the world—and back home in the states—it's a pretty safe bet that a person is just drawn to it."

"So were you?" Soli asks. "Drawn to shamanism, I mean?"

"Yes. But at the time, like most people who feel that pull in the West, I didn't know that it was shamanism I was being drawn to. At first, I just knew that I could usually tell where another person was hurting or what the mood was when I entered a room. Things that I assumed anyone could do if they only paid attention." I realize that I am feeling very contented. The food is excellent and I'm being quizzed on one of my favorite subjects. Life is good!

"But even then, I was awful at things like reading people's minds or getting objects to move without touching them." Soli nods, listening intently.

"That was supposed to be funny…" Soli cocks her head and I see that she wants me to focus. "The thing is, it took me years to get through my own blocks to the point where I could even begin to trust my own intuition, and that's essential to working as a shaman."

I look up to see the German couple crossing the street now, the husband's body language expressing his victory, while the wife's expresses her defeat. Soli turns over her shoulder to see what's distracting me, and turns back with a satisfied smile.

She leans toward me conspiratorially as the BMW pulls out of the car park and purrs away. "I think she had an affair with the fellow who's getting married, and I think she was hoping to 'renew their acquaintance' by staying at the chateau—they were arguing about taking a room in town, but nothing was available now. However, thanks to modern technology," she leans back and smiles smugly, "I was able to find them a B&B just out of town."

"Wasn't that kind of mean?" I suggest.

Soli drops her smile. "She deserves it. She shouldn't be fooling around anyway."

Obviously done with that subject, Soli consults her notes again. "I'm confused about what you just said. Didn't you have teachers? Didn't they help you with all of that?"

"I wish I had. But most of the 'teachers' I tried to learn from ...well, it didn't work very well. It always seemed like they weren't quite what I was looking for. To this day, I don't know how much of it was their ego and how much was mine, but someone's ego got in the way. I was so skeptical. Anytime someone wanted to sell me on their particular map, I would immediately get turned off. I would begin questioning the validity of the map even before I had learned it. I suppose that made me a pretty difficult student as well. But there was more to it than that. I knew at some level that the kind of teaching I needed was not informational but experiential."

"You make it sound like having a teacher is a waste of time."

"Having a good teacher is invaluable. But to me, a good teacher is one that tries to get you to find the information yourself—through experience. Shamanism isn't a compact discipline, like math or science. There are very few—if any—hard facts to learn, so it's really more like getting to know your way around a new neighborhood. It takes time. The best teachers are more like native guides. But as I said, teaching alone isn't enough. Even the best of teachers can't make someone a shaman."

Soli nods and takes this in for a moment before replying. "I don't mean to be stupid, but just what is it that does make someone a shaman? I don't think I understand that."

I wish I really knew the answer to that myself. I take another sip of coffee and try to tap into some deeper source of wisdom for her. After a moment, I just say what comes to mind—hoping it will make sense. "You know how I love analogy. Sometimes I think it's really the only way to get a handle on this stuff. So let's take a look at what it takes to become a fighter pilot in the Air Force. First, you have to have the interest. Second, you have to have the physical, mental and psychological profiles that make the Air Force willing to invest in your training. Finally, you have to be able to learn everything they have to teach you and practice it proficiently. Becoming a shaman, you don't have to deal with the Air Force, of course, but you do have to deal with the spirits..."

Soli grimaces, "You realize of course that even talking about spirits makes me—and most others—immediately doubt everything you say."

"Yes—that's one of the major hurdles to doing this work. It might help to think of these spirits as psychological allegories for the moment—just to get past them. To return to my analogy..."

"Okay."

"You need to have the interest in doing the work, the ability or talent to do the work and you have to pass the tests of the spirits–"

"Tests of spirits! That sounds fascinating," Soli smiles. "As long as by 'spirits' you mean psychological allegories. What sort of tests—and what happens if you don't pass?"

I shake my head, half remembering the various hoops I jumped through without really knowing why at the time. "They can be almost anything. There could be a test of will, as in: can you stay up all night long dancing around a bonfire just because you promised the spirits that you would? They can be tests of insight—where opportunities appear out of nowhere and you have to be able to make a snap decision, or you lose your chance. And they're often tests of your seriousness. Like: Are you ready to engage and deal with the really terrifying shadows that you have to pass through on your way to being a shaman?"

Soli is slowly nodding. Her eyes are focused inward and she's not taking notes at this point, so I continue. "You have to be willing to be transformed into something other than what you think you are. Or perhaps allow your true nature to be revealed to you. Either way, it's not a fun process. It usually involves an experience of death and dismemberment; death of the ego of course, but it doesn't feel like that when it's happening. It's easily the most terrifying experience I've had, and if it weren't for the fact that I'm more happy and fulfilled afterward than before, I couldn't recommend it to anyone."

Soli seems perplexed—but not convinced. "If all that is true, then why would anyone do it?"

"I can't speak for everyone, but for myself, it seems like some of us just have the need—or the obsession—to shamanize. Like you have the constant need to turn everything into work; another project or another script—even that cheap novel you're reading. This is just a different need—to journey beyond what we think of as 'reality.' Just like some people become fighter pilots, in spite of all the difficulties, because nothing else will be true for them."

I can see that she is almost getting it. "It's not that teachers are completely useless. There are many things you can and have to learn from teachers. But you also have to realize eventually that only the process of life can teach you the deepest lessons. That only your inner teachers can reach deep enough into you to see the things you can't—and awaken them to where you can see them. The most effective shamans—and shamanic teachers—realize that what they are doing is helping the person they teach to stir up the hidden resources of their own souls—to re–member the whole Self. I think the best I can do—as a teacher myself—is to intuitively respond to my students in the way that works for them. I have to be able to recognize when it's time to leave off with my teaching and let them start learning directly from the experience itself."

I seem to be losing her again. "Okay. I've gotten a bit off track here. What happens if you don't pass the tests is that you don't become a shaman. And the reason for doing it—for taking on the tests and the terror and all of that—is just that nothing else feels...right. Nothing else fills that hollow place inside you—or answers that call or longing within you."

She taps her front teeth with her stylus again and looks at me as if she is trying to decide whether or not I'm being straight with her. "Alright. I still don't feel like I'm getting the whole story though. If you didn't learn much from the teachers you didn't like, then how did you learn to be a shaman?"

I finish the last bite of the excellent croissant and wash it down with the cooling dregs of my coffee. "Now you'll really think I'm crazy, but the best teacher I've ever had is one of those. . . psychological allegories I was talking about.

Deepening

When I look at my journey so far along the path of shamanism, it is difficult to say who is and who is not a "teacher". This is made more difficult by my own internal resistance to teachers. Because of the various traumas of my early life—all well in keeping with traditional shamanic initiation—I have found it difficult to accept anyone being "bigger" than me. This makes it hard to accept anyone as an effective teacher. Instead, I learned a great deal through books and even more from direct experience– also known as making lots of mistakes.

In spite of all the difficulties, there are a few teachers and mentors I've had who were excellent and who helped me tremendously. The most important to me is Elisheva: The Shofet of a form of primitive Hebrew earth spirituality called AmCHa Aretz. She has been my mentor and teacher for more than 20 years. I don't believe that she has ever referred to herself as a shaman. Just as any healer or seer from a traditional society would, she sticks with the terminology of her own culture. From Elisheva I have learned more than I could possibly put into words. Part of it though comes down to learning a way of being. By learning to know myself–the full spectrum including both light and dark–I find myself much more able to really See others.

There are others. Doctor Guao taught me the essentials of Chinese Medicine and Medical QiGong, long before I realized that this was another form of shamanism. Master William Ting, who taught me how to bring so much of what I have learned into my body and energy through Tai Chi, Qigong and Pushing Hands. More recently, I have studied with Heinz Stark, who is a master of a form of group shamanism called Systemic Constellation Work and also a shaman, bodyworker and artist in his own right.

For me, the hardest part of explaining about my teachers is acknowledging that, when it comes to the shamanic work that I practice and teach, I really had no formal teachers. Back in the late 70's and early 80's I worked a lot with creative visualization, hypnosis and NLP, before being introduced to Harner's "Way of the Shaman." In all of these practices, I felt that something important was missing. Intuitively, I knew that I was looking for something that had to be there, and so I kept looking on my own until I created the techniques I now use. In short, no other person actually taught me about how to connect with spirits; how to journey; how to reach into another person's body with my energy to help them to heal–all of this came before I was really able to accept another's influence over me as a teacher. And this has been a large part of my unique journey of becoming a shaman. This is not easy for me to speak to, because there is still that part of me that believes that things of value come only from others. And yet, this is the very wound that is being healed by acknowledging the validity and strength of my work–both with myself and others.

Many of the shaman's best teachers arise after they have already taken on the role and begun their shamanic work. These teachers are the patients who come to us with wounds that we can only heal be growing ourselves; the students who ask questions we don't know the answers to; the colleagues who push us to go beyond our own fears.

How does someone who has the "gift," the need to serve as a shaman, go about becoming a shaman? The easy answer is pretty Zen: You just allow your true nature to manifest. If your true nature is to be a shaman, then you will be.

The fact is that we live in a world of schools, tests, certificates and standards for judging everything from doctors to cars. It is very hard to leave these things behind and still operate effectively with people who live in the midst of it all. We often feel that we have to have some piece of paper on the wall that says we are "okay." For some it's a medical license; for others, a ministerial certificate. But there is no certification for a practicing shaman other than the effectiveness of their own work. I can't acknowledge someone as a shaman just because they've taken all my workshops, read this book, and journeyed into the three worlds of the shaman. I need to know that they can, and will, serve effectively in the role of the shaman. This means being able to work in service to their community while maintaining their own practice of growth, healing and awakening. This will look different from one person to the next. For some it may be having a private practice where they work with individuals who require healing or spiritual growth work that is not to be found elsewhere. For others it might mean taking on one or more of the tradition roles of the shaman in community–the one who reminds us of who we are, where we come from, how we belong and how we fit into the world we live in.

Here's the slightly less zen answer: The way a person becomes a shaman now—in the modern world—is very much the way they always have. Their lives are shaped by the experiences of their childhood and later life, in such a way that the inner core is shaken awake and shown possibilities beyond the ordinary.

If the person has the strength, and resolve, necessary to engage these possibilities and explore the larger world and, if they have the need to use their abilities to serve community in this role, then they become a shaman. It's not something anyone can do for you; it's a natural emergence of the inevitable.

My best example of this process is in my own life. I was born into a family of fundamentalist, Old Testament Christians. We were fed the idea that we were the modern, spiritual equivalent of the Jews and that we would be persecuted, just like the Jews have always been. According to the church, by 1975 the world as we knew it would come to an end; Germany would rise again and a time of Tribulations would come. They were quite graphic in their descriptions of these tribulations, relying heavily on stories from the Holocaust. The impact of this on me was that by the time I was ten, every time a civil defense siren went off, I would have a panic attack, running outside to watch the sky for the German paratroopers.

I had one older brother–John–who had cystic fibrosis, a terminal disease that left him looking like a refugee from the WWII concentration camps and added to the whole atmosphere of living under the shadow of death. He died when I was six years old. I don't recall feeling much of anything.

My mother was talented, high maintenance, overweight and chronically ill. As a child, all I knew was that she was my mother and that I wanted her to love me. Unfortunately, her boundaries were not always the best. She died when I was ten. I don't recall feeling much of anything.

My father was a traveling salesman, selling pens, business cards, calendars and anything you could print your name on all throughout central and northern Arizona. Despite his charm and charisma, he was probably chronically depressed. He was an alcoholic, but not a mean one. When he came home from work, he would have a few beers "to relax"–and would smile distantly at any attempt to engage. He was a WWII vet, and though he would never talk about his experiences in the war, he had all the signs of what I've come to know as Post Traumatic Stress Disorder—or Veteran's Syndrome. He died when I was 14 and I was left with my younger sister. I assumed I would be responsible for her–as I had already been for several years. I don't remember feeling much of anything.

By the time my sister and I were moved to Cincinnati to live with my mother's sister, I was pretty numb. I stayed that way through high school and into my early years of college. It was during this period in my early 20's that I began waking up a bit and looking at things like Magick, Buddhism, Meditation, Yoga, Martial Arts and Shamanism as a means of responding to the pain and rage that had accumulated inside. It was also also about that time that I was diagnosed with acute Post Traumatic Stress Disorder.

There is a clear rule in modern psychotherapy against sharing your own personal story with your clients. This rule does not always hold true when doing shamanic/soul-level work. There are times when the clients need to see that the person they are trusting to lead them through the sometimes dark and terrifying landscape of their inner self has had some experience with similar terrain before–and made it through to the other side in one piece.

These early experiences helped to give me the depth I needed to serve as a trustworthy guide for others. They helped to shape me as a person and as a shaman. But it was my response to the traumas that made all the difference. Instead of becoming a victim, I became a survivor–and eventually much more than that. Anyone can have a traumatic childhood. It is what we DO with this "gift" that opens the way to shamanic awakening. In many ways, these early experiences reflect the sort of "initiations" referred to by Eliade and others in their descriptions of traditional shamanism. However, since I was not born into a culture that has a context for shamanic initiation or practice, it is only in retrospect that this connection becomes clear.

One of the first tests of a shaman is to heal themselves. We accomplish this only with a great deal of help. This healing forms the foundation of what we offer to others in our work as a shaman.

Chapter 4
Rocks

After a good night's sleep at a B&B in Bayeux and breakfast in another outdoor cafe overlooking the oceanfront, I am feeling ready to continue our journey. We have switched drivers and I am a little intimidated by the idea of driving in France. Soli is navigating, so if we get lost, it's not my fault. In any case, we are making good time. I am admiring the smoothly banked curves and wide shoulders of the motorway, built on the ruins of some ancient Roman road no doubt, with the intention of lasting until some future civilization is ready to look at us as we look back at the Romans.

I am beginning to feel a bit frustrated again with not being able to learn the little bit of French necessary to read the road signs, when I see one that I do understand. It's a white silhouette of standing stones against a brown field—an international symbol for a stone circle, and a very pleasing sight for me.

Pulling us off the exit, I realize that my sudden change of direction must have jostled Soli, and yet, when I glance over at her, she seems to not have noticed anything. Her feet are braced against the dash and her Mac laptop is open on her knees. Just as I think I may be able to surprise her by getting us somewhere without her help, she speaks up. "Navigator to helm: Are you sure you know where you are taking us?"

It seems Soli is in a good mood. I don't know if there's any reason for it, but I'm not complaining. "Well—" I reply. "You did suggest that we follow the signs and you did ask for a more thorough explanation of sacred space. I thought this might do the trick."

"And what is 'this?'" Soli asks.

"Oh—just some rocks."

"Shamans!" she snorts, but she is smiling as she shakes her head and returns to her laptop. Her fingers clattering away on the computer keys dance with the voice of the wheels on the road, creating a strange and hypnotic sort of music. It occurs to me that these are the sort of rhythmic sounds that could open doorways between the worlds.

A few more kilometers down the winding country road, I slow down as I spy a large sheet of slate with the single word, "rocks," scrawled in white paint, propped up against a tree. Parking the car on the muddy shoulder of the road, we climb out. Soli stows her computer away in the back and changes into her hiking boots and wraps her woolen cape around her, then we follow the arrow on the sign.

The path leads us through a band of trees and through a meadow filled with soft green ferns. There is a slightly swampy odor coming from the far edge of the field that seems in contrast to the sense of beauty and grace that fills my vision.

I wait for Soli to break out of her thoughts during our walk, but she is still silent when we arrive at a worn information booth that looks like it hasn't been open for several seasons. Pulling a weathered brochure from a stack held down with a rock, I begin reading about Le Pays de Guer-Coetquidan: a stone circle that also holds the 9th century chapel of St. Nicolas. Finding an outcropping of granite, Soli rests against millenium-old stone in her brilliant red cape, the deep green moss running down the stone like rivulets of water, and I think that this was a better idea than I could have imagined. I know that Soli has been feeling uncomfortable in her own skin lately. Something is tugging at her from within, and that's enough to put anyone on edge.

Looking around, I can feel the spirit of the place welcoming us, penetrating through earth and stone, and I think to myself how spirit is always attracted to beauty. I look over at Soli as she smiles back at me. She's still not ready to talk, but I feel like I have a glimpse of her own inner beauty that is rising in response to this sacred place.

We move past the information booth. Off to one side of the stones, there is a recreation in miniature of a megalithic settlement, not that much taller than Soli and I, strewn with old newspapers. She raises her eyebrows at me as if it ask, Is this sacred?

The model illustrates just how the ancients may have raised the stones, and we stop only briefly. It seems that both the booth and the accompanying exhibits have been abandoned. We have the place entirely to ourselves.

Partially excavated, the stones are protected with yellow plastic caution tape, but the main area is still accessible. While Soli stands at the edge of the excavation, I approach slowly, even cautiously, listening on more than one level for any clues, cues, or signs of how to proceed. Soli looks around as if expecting a gendarme to show up and cart us away for trespassing on a site of ancient relics.

A faint boundary of sacred space still exists here. According to the artist's sketch at the information booth, a double ring of stones once stood here. More than a thousand years later, only a scattering remain; some fallen, others sinking deeply into the moist earth. Somehow the circle has maintained a great presence despite its loss of form, still towering over our heads, even in its chaotic maze.

One slender stone calls to me, standing alone in the outer circle. It's worn light on one side, dark on the other, and I know intuitively that this stone will serve as my gateway. It strikes me that I will only be able to enter this space by leaving my modern self behind. I begin by emptying my pockets and removing my wristwatch, placing the coins, wallet and watch on the ground beside me. Leaning my forehead and the palms of my hands against the stone's sun-warmed face, I ask wordlessly for permission to enter. After a few slow minutes, I feel a sliding sensation under my hands and, in my shamanic body, the stone moves open like a sliding double door and I step through, leaving my physical body behind.

Even after 20 years of practice, this process is still peculiar. Perhaps the only way to describe it is stepping into a lucid dream while still very much aware of the sensations of my physical body. Somewhere in my consciousness I hold a cord connecting me to the physical, and it's comforting to know that my body is waiting for me. I can even feel my head resting against the cooling stone.

The sensation of coming fully back into my physical body is subtle. It feels like I've been watching two channels on a television and one channel has suddenly been turned off. I have no idea how long I've been gone, but the sun has shifted lower and the air has cooled. I push myself away from the stone, stretching the stiffness from my back. My head is pounding slightly as I retrieve my watch and other cargo from the ground and stand to stuff it back into my pockets. As I do so, I notice that Soli is perched on a nearby rock, almost glaring at me. "What is it?" I ask.

"What on earth were you doing—contemplating your navel?" She frowns as if checking me for signs of dementia.

"Not quite." I laugh. "I just went on a little journey, and got more than I bargained for." I go on to tell her what I have just experienced.

"As I passed through the stone, day turned into night filled with a hundred flickering torches. There was a crowd of people—a tribe —watching me. A short, stocky fellow—I think maybe he was a priest—with grizzled, grey hair and beard came up to me wearing a long tunic of rough brown cloth. He stopped right in front of me, looking deep into my eyes, as if he was making sure of me in some way.

"When he began speaking, I knew I was in someone else's body, because the person whose body I was using could still understand what the priest was saying and responded in what must have been the same language. I didn't understand any of it, but it struck me as very formal—almost like a ritual. I got a sense that the person who's body I was visiting was aware of me too. Even though I didn't understand the language they used, I still got the gist of what they were saying—that the priest fellow was asking me why I was there, and I told him that I was there to create a bond between our peoples. He motioned for me to follow and led me a short distance through the stones to where a bonfire blazed at the center of the stone ring. There were huge fir trees, at least 60 feet tall, maybe more, all around the stones, reflecting the light of the fire. Beneath the trees were even more people, standing there watching us.

"Standing at the fire he asked me to state my intentions again, handing me a large horn filled with drink. Raising the horn high, I spoke so that all the people there could hear me over the roar of the fire, "Let our ancestors be your ancestors...let your ancestors be our ancestors!" Then I poured a bit of the drink into the flames and drank the rest as the voices chanted "Halldess, halldess, halldess..." Those were the only words I can remember, and I have no clue what they meant, but it felt something like 'hail the gods.'

"There was one other thing. When I looked down at the fire, I saw three lizards looking back at me, all twined together somehow in the flames. That seemed the most interesting to me, as if it was the message I was there to receive. Then I turned myself around— moved out of whoever's body it was—and came back here, feeling like I had done what I had come there to do. Almost as if I was finishing a job that I had started a long, long time ago. If I was going to try to make some sense of it, I would say that I traveled back to a past life, into a place where I should have gone in that life, and completed a task that I was supposed to have done then. It was actually quite satisfying."

Soli is silent for a moment, then suddenly flares. "How nice for you!" she replies, in a tone that lets me know she is just short of stamping her feet and throwing things.

At a loss for anything else to say, I ask "What are you feeling right now?"

She glares at me. "Nothing!" she snaps, but then drops some of her intensity. "Well—not completely nothing. I felt the stones, ran my fingers over them, and each one felt a little different—somehow. But then this feeling came up that this place is familiar. Not like

I've been here before, but as if I was supposed to be here. As if—
and I suppose this makes me sound as crazy as you—as if I was
shown this place on a map, had it described to me, and that I was
supposed to have come here, but never did." It's apparent she's
not feeling anything but rage, but just as clearly, the rage is
covering something deeper.

I walk over to her and kneel beside the stone. She turns away from
me, won't look at me; instead she gazes into the grass, eyes
unfocused and glossy with unshed tears.

"Why don't you tell me about it?" I coax, my voice pitched low
and soft, gentle and calm. I think she might sob or explode, and it's
hard to tell which will come first.

Deepening

The inner world I pass through while journeying is completely
accessible by others as well. It may seem unreachable to your
thinking self, but it is not. It lies just within you.

Here's a helpful exercise: Imagine you're standing outside of a
large building. Take a look at it. Imagine the size, color, the texture
of it. What is the architecture—the time period? How many
windows does it have? How many doors? Does your building
stand close to the street or in the middle of a field? Is it surrounded
by grass, wilderness, or interesting characters who roam about it?

Now go to the door of this building. Reach out and touch it. What
sort of doorknob does it have? How does it feel beneath your
fingers? Turn the knob, open the door and walk through. You are

inside this building now. Feel what it is like to be contained, embraced by this building. Begin to explore. Take your time, discovering each room, one after another, like climbing a spiral staircase, until you arrive at the center. Here, in an open space, there is a single door within a seemingly solid wall, but the wall becomes invisible. As you try to walk around the door to see the other side, the door turns with you, always facing you.

Now reach out, open the door, and step through. You might feel a curious sensation as you move through the door. Just pay attention to that. Coming through the other side, it seems as if you have simply turned around and faced the same door again, as if you traveled nowhere. The room around you looks like the room you just left, and yet it feels subtly different. Moving away from the door, you explore this building as well. While it is similar to the building you just left, it is not quite the same.

Find your way back to the center again. Go to the door, and move through it, once again noting the sensation of moving through the doorway and returning to that first building. You may leave the door open, or close it, as you will. Move out of the building, turn around, and look back.

This building is your physical body. The doorway at the center of the building leads to your inner body. This introduces a dimension that we don't usually deal with in our everyday lives. This is the dimension of inwardness, which is like a reflection of the outer.

This dimension is as important to the practicing shaman as the dimensions of width and height are to a carpenter. It allows us access to a whole spectrum beyond the physical. This is the inner landscape that I've referred to in the previous chapters. This is the inner world which is extended through the doorway to overlap with the outer world, creating the threshold state that allows us to recognize omens.

Go ahead and try the simple exercise described above, realizing that the building you are entering is your physical body, and that you are moving through that doorway at your center into a different body. Pay particular attention to any sensation you may experience while passing through that doorway. When you have the exercise down, it will be easy to translate it to moving into that same doorway in the center of your physical body, without needing the imaginary building to guide you.

We all have this inner doorway. We all inhabit this inner world. You can learn to move into and through this world at will, just as you do the outer world you think of as reality.

Chapter 5
Swallowed by Stones

"Guilty." Soli says finally. "I feel very guilty. And I have no idea why!" At this she stands abruptly and walks over to the nearest standing stone, facing it as if it were a wall. I stay where I am, careful not to distract her. At the same time, I begin drawing energy around her, weaving a cocoon of light to help her to contain her thoughts and feelings. While it takes considerable concentration, it's one of the most powerful means of helping someone gain clarity; what was before a fragmented memory or feeling becomes more whole. I am hoping that Soli will get a clearer picture of the emotional response triggered by the stones— possibly an unresolved issue from a past life. It seems to be working, as she turns and looks back at me, obviously in a light trance.

"I'm too late,"she says.

"Too late for what?"

"I don't know. Something important!" Soli begins to pace now, moving slowly back and forth between two stones. "I feel as if I am getting garbled bits of an important message, and I can't find the rest of it. All I know is that it's important and I've missed it! I feel like a little girl who is late for lunch and all the food is gone or she's on a bus tour with her class, and the bus has left without her..."

Surprised by the image, I laugh.

"It's not funny!" Soli flares. "I hate to miss things!"

I nod and she lowers her head again.

"I'm sorry. I don't know what's wrong with me...or why I feel so awful. Let's just go." Her eyes are glimmering but she seems incapable of actually crying.

We stand and begin to walk slowly back toward the entrance, passing by the freshly excavated stones. Here Soli pauses. She seems drawn to the recently emerged stones. It is as if they hold something for her. It occurs to me that Soli is in quite an altered state right now, but she doesn't realize it and isn't at all used to it. At the moment though, she looks lost, sad, and guilty. Like a scolded child.

She turns to me. "What can I do?" she asks.

"Perhaps there's something unfinished for you here too," I nod towards the stones behind the yellow tape. "You could take some time to acknowledge that connection and to...apologize? For whatever it is that you might have done—or not done." I know that I am talking to some deeper part of her than the one I have been driving through France with. This deeper part seems to clarify for a moment and she turns and steps over the tape, walking to a place in the stones where they overhang a deep pool of water. There she crouches for a minute or so. Then she deliberately tears a single button from the front of her blouse, holds it for a moment as if whispering to it in her hand, and then tosses it into the dark water. When she stands again, she seems to have given up. Still frustrated, she steps back across the caution tape and stands with her arms crossed. She stays there for a minute, looking at the ground. Finally she stirs and looks up at me, with a small wry smile.

"Quite the shamaness aren't I? I can't even get rid of my own yuck."

"It's always hardest to do the work on yourself," I tell her. "And besides, you're not a shaman yet. And I didn't realize you were interested in becoming one." I smile to take the sting out of my words, but it feels important that she realizes that it just isn't that easy to become a shaman.

Taking her by the hand, I lead her back across the tape and to the side of the pool. I sit down on the rock and after a moment's hesitation she joins me. "I don't want to push you into this." She stares at me blankly—resentfully? "It could trigger emotions that you've managed to store away for quite some time now. But I know that you don't want to carry this around with you for the rest of the day. I certainly don't want you to. So do you mind if I help you to dump some of that yuck?"

After a moment's consideration, she nods again. I reach over and place my hand on her back near her heart center. "Now—just breathe for a bit."

Her back is warm under my touch and I use my energy to ask permission from her soul for us to work together. Slowly she lets my energy in. It feels like she is trusting me more and I want to treat that trust with gentleness and respect. Part of the work I do is about bringing things into harmony or union. In order to do this, I need to be able to feel how they are—and where they need to move to. Much of this I do by feeling the rhythms; the physical, energetic pulse moving within and around the person. So I begin by feeling for the rhythm of her breath, and beneath that, the rhythm of her heart beat, and beneath that, the rhythm of her qi, flowing in and out through her center. Her heart is pounding and her breath forced; every rhythm is out of sync with the others. I begin to resonate with her, to set up a deep, gentle vibration with my voice and energy, that moves through me and into her as well. I tune the resonance to draw her deeper into her center and thus into a deeper relaxation, letting go of some of the stress and frustration. As I feel her heartbeat calm and her breathing slow, I deepen the resonance even more, focusing on the slower and more unified rhythms of my own pulses. This brings her different rhythms closer to mine–and allows us to move deeper together. Her eyes flutter closed and her body relaxes even more. She is ready.

The dark water waits expectantly beneath us, both literally and figuratively, and I now use the resonance of my voice out loud, in a quiet overtone, to open a way for us to dive below the surface into the cooling depths—the depths of the water and of Soli—that lie undisturbed beneath her rapidly calming emotions. Soli's tension dissipates even more quickly now, while deeper parts of her blossom open, drinking in the soothing quiet here beneath the water. Her body relaxes, her breath calm now, her face softened.

Gently, I coax the knots of Soli's fear to open more by reaching more deeply into her body with my own qi, sending sensations of relaxation and release. We have many layers to our beings–much more than simply body, mind and spirit. There are bodies that we wear in dreams and in other journeys, that our minds have no awareness of. She is drifting down beneath her conscious self, between her Dream Body and even deeper parts of herself. I've not worked with her like this before. Our few chances to do altered states work at Mystery School were very superficial, and I don't know what to expect as I begin unwinding the layers of memory and other substance. Dark and vivid forms, like figures from a dream, begin to stir within her and one strong figure works its way free.

I find myself joined by this new presence. It is a strong, feminine essence—something like a priestess or sorceress. Her eyes carry green light and I can feel her seeing me as well as I see her. Focusing more clearly into my shamanic body, I open my hands in greeting. She cocks her head to the side in response, observing me with a mild curiosity that soon turns into recognition. "Ah," she finally speaks, slowly, in a deep-timbered whisper, like someone who is still dreaming. "So you are the one who answered the call." I respond with silence, waiting for her to state her intention. "It's time for me to awaken," she says.

I hesitate to respond to that. It seems a very loaded situation—one that I didn't come here for, at least not consciously. But it also lets me know, in no uncertain terms, that there is deeper work underway here—and apparently I am involved.

I ask her if she has something to resolve here, something that Soli needs to do in order to let go of the grief and pain she is feeling. The green-eyed lady moves and I can see her reaching into the shadows and untying something, then she leans closer and seems to blow into Soli's heart. There is a palpable shift in the energy, as if the atmosphere has suddenly become more dense. The green-eyed woman straightens and looks at me with a smile before flickering like a candle flame in a breeze and disappearing.

Her departure is like an anchor dropping away, and I find myself rising quickly back to the surface—back to my ordinary state of consciousness and into my physical form once more. Slowing my ascent, I take hold of Soli as well, breathing both of us back through the center and into the outer world. Opening my eyes, I see that Soli is still deeply relaxed, her eyes still shut, on the verge of sleep.

Using my voice once more, I draw her back toward her ordinary consciousness. I begin with a deeply resonant tone and once I feel it engaging her awareness and joining at the same frequency, I begin slowly raising the tone until it matches with my current state of awareness. She emerges naturally and her eyes flicker open as she sits up. Looking around, she seems a bit confused at first. "Did I fall asleep?"

"No. Not really. How do you feel?"

Soli starts to answer then hesitates, as if searching for something she expected to find and not finding it. Finally she smiles and answers. "Much better! Thank you. Whatever you did got rid of all that yuck I was feeling."

Standing and stretching, I reply, "I'm not really sure that I had much to do with that."

"What do you mean? Of course you did! All I did was throw away a perfectly good button…." She looks down at her blouse, "… which I will now need to replace."

I am not sure what to tell Soli about my encounter with her deeper self. In fact, I'm not even entirely sure what to make of the experience myself. As the sensations of the journey fade, it's much like awakening from a dream, and the dream is beginning to fade. At least, if the journey was valid, I know that some level of Soli's awareness is engaged in the process.

Looking into the slate blue sky, I close my eyes and extend my awareness a bit into the surrounding landscape. A presence still rests beneath our feet. Perhaps it is the female figure I just glimpsed in my work with Soli. Perhaps not. In any case, she does not rise to my gentle probing, so I withdraw.

Before heading back toward the car, I squat down in front of the doorway stone and dig into my jacket pocket for the package of tobacco I carry for such occasions. I leave a pinch of tobacco at the foot of the stone, as an offering of thanks to the spirits that still occupy this place.

Deepening

Stillness is the inner doorway through which the transformation process emerges—a doorway to the depths. Without stillness, these depths remain obscured by turbulent emotions. Stillness is one of the simplest, most fascinating techniques I know. You find it at the root of every effective mystical pursuit. It is the act of letting go of the attachment to everything you know, allowing the mind to become formless—wordless. Dropping into your center, you find your doorway. That doorway is your outer, your physical body. This is another way of looking at the same doorway discussed in the last deepening.

Try it. See what happens. Close your eyes. Feel your body. Acknowledge what thoughts and sensations are there—and let them go. The thoughts may continue, so let them. It's like walking out of a room where a radio is playing. Thoughts are only a distraction if you focus on them. Let them fall into the background as you plummet deeper into your self—following gravity inward to that one center that allows you to access the inner world.

As you come to a stop on your inward journey, ask yourself "Is this as deep as I can go? Can this inner gravity take me deeper?" If you can go deeper, let it happen. This means that you have not yet reached the door. If you cannot—if the answer is "no"—then you have reached the door.

Go to the door and open it. Don't go through just yet. For now, just sit down and watch. Maybe something will come through the door. Then again, perhaps not. It doesn't matter. You are the observer. If something does appear, just acknowledge it, let it pass you, and keep watching the open door.

Stay here for as long as you feel comfortable, then a little longer. Eventually allow yourself to rise back up into your thoughts and ego. As you open your eyes back in your physical body, in the outer building, check the clock. How long have you spent watching the door?

Everything else that you do on your spiritual journey is based on the foundation of Stillness. Stillness provides the doorway into the transformations that arise from and during this journey.

Stillness is one of the foundation practices that I offer clients when they come to me searching for spiritual growth. It also helps them to get more out of their sessions of shamanic work. With practice, they are able to enter into Stillness more easily and effectively, which allows me to work with them more deeply.

Having introduced the practice of Stillness as a means of accessing the inner world, I would like to move on to a very important question: Why would someone in our modern society seek out a shaman? The best answer I can come up with is that someone seeks out a shaman because their soul recognizes the need for healing or growth that will require some outside assistance. This can look like anything from plantar fasciitis to tennis elbow, when the client first appears. However, somewhere in the first few sessions, it becomes clear that there is some other issue in need of attention.

This deeper issue may involve any number of old or new traumas, most likely dating back to early childhood. Often the healing process can begin with retrieving some part of the self or soul that was cut off from the rest of the self by the traumatic event. This process of "soul or power retrieval" is fundamental to the work shamans do with their clients.

With my own clients, I do my best to engage them in this process, so that it is not me retrieving the missing pieces for them. Instead, they are assisting in the process— fully engaged in their own healing—so that it becomes an empowerment on more than one level.

As these first sessions with a client proceed, there are often some powerful transformations that begin to take place as deeper parts of their soul begin to respond to the sensation of being engaged and seen by someone outside of the self. Strong emotional releases often occur as the soul shakes loose from sleep and becomes more involved in the conscious life of the client.

It is impossible to really describe this process, as it is so deeply internal, personal and intimate to the individual. Though it often includes episodes of ecstatic joy, there are just as often periods of stark terror and depression.

The process varies dramatically as clients progress, but generally speaking, they experience a greater sense of well-being and security in their self; a sense of belonging in their life; more connection with their ancestors; and, a growing awareness that there is much more to them than they ever suspected. Some have realized gifts that they were born with, which had been repressed their whole life. Others have simply felt their "whole self" returned to them so that they can proceed with their lives. And some few have actually connected with their own need to be in service to others as clergy, counselors, healers or—dare I say—shamans.

Chapter 6
Blood on the Road

In lieu of any obvious synchronicity, we have decided to treat the
stones at Monteneuf as an indication that we should look for other
sacred stones, and so we are heading vaguely in the direction of
Carnac, which has one of the largest stone alignments in the world.
I expect to feel some sort of anticipation, and yet I feel oddly
uninspired. It's as if the decision to head for Carnac is not quite
"it"—not the path of synchronicity. This is what often happens
when I respond from my head rather than my instincts.
Unfortunately, my instincts are keeping quiet for the moment.

As we wind our way through the rolling hills and brilliant green of
the French countryside, it becomes clear that even beauty can
become monotonous after awhile. I am focusing on the sensation
of my body leaning from one side to the other as the car sways into
the curves. Is my body's movement guiding the car, or is the car
moving my body? Are both guiding each other? There is
something very regular, almost rhythmic—even hypnotic—to the
snake–like turns, lulling me into a gentle trance.

It occurs to me that I am driving and that it would be best to stay
awake and alert for that. This thought arises just as I come round a
bend and see flashing brake lights right in front of me. I brake hard
and swerve onto the shoulder of the road, narrowly missing a
green van. The lights of emergency vehicles make staccato blasts of
white and blue from beyond the line of cars in front of us.

Looking over at Soli, I see that the commotion has shaken her out
of her nest of novel, notebook and pillow. She is holding the
handle at the top of her door in a white knuckled grip and staring

at the van beside her. I think she is trying to catch up with the abrupt change in conditions. After all, a moment ago we were driving calmly through a sleepy countryside and suddenly we are surrounded by stopped cars, emergency lights and apparent chaos.

"Now I see why you don't complain about my driving." Soli shudders and slowly releases her vise grip on the door handle.

Her words feel unfair to me. After all, I think I've just done an great job of keeping us from getting smashed up. However, I don't think that biting Soli's head off is going to help, so I just take a few deep breaths and let my heart rate settle back down. This is one of the many residual effects of post traumatic stress disorder that I still have to deal with. Any shock triggers an adrenal reaction all out of proportion to the actual event. I know that for awhile now I will be absolutely calm on the outside, able to cope with whatever happens. It will only be 20 minutes or so before I start to shake a bit around the edges and feel sick to my stomach.

When I look back, Soli has already returned to entering notes on her Palm Pilot. Why she uses her notebook for some things and her Palm for others, I've no idea. She seems to have picked up her thread of thought from before I so rudely interrupted by bringing us to such an abrupt stop. "This is going to make a terrific film," she proclaims, waving the novel in her hand. "Of course, it's not very well written, but that will be fixed in the screenplay. It's a moving story though, with a powerful female character—Dahut, the daughter of the local king—who angers the local bishop by refusing to convert to Christianity. When her father does convert, she has him build her a city of her own called Ys, where she will move with her fellow pagans."

Putting the Mercedes into reverse, I ease us back onto the pavement in between the green van and one of the small Euro cars that all look alike to me at the moment. We move forward slowly, in fits and starts. Soli finally finishes her notes and turns her curiosity to the situation at hand. She pops her door open, and hops out of the slowly rolling car, thumping the door shut behind her. This seems out of character for her but for all I know, it's yet another mysterious European custom—perhaps their version of the Chinese fire drill.

I have pulled to a stop—again—behind another van, when Soli returns, climbing in and slamming the door shut. She seems shaken. "It looks like an accident, but I don't see a wreck. There's just a police car and an ambulance," she reports. "And a body." We inch past, slowed by the rubber-necking of other drivers.

The police car is pulled completely off the road and the officer—gendarme—is directing traffic while a couple of men in white coveralls lift a black body bag on a gurney into the back of the ambulance. I glance out the open window and notice that we are passing through a wide reddish stain. I feel a twinge of discomfort —as if someone is shoving me through an unexpected doorway— and then a curious combination of grief and gratitude, though I don't know what for—a lightness and a heaviness all at once. I glance over and see that Soli is gazing out her window at the bloodstain we've just driven through. Then we are entering an intersection and the way ahead is blocked by a police van with another gendarme directing the line of cars to detour to the left onto a road marked "Quiberon."

"I guess we are going this way then," I say as the Officer emphatically directs us through the turn. As the traffic begins to return to normal, I find myself wanting to distance myself from the feelings as well. With a brief curiosity as to what is so uncomfortable about them, I leave them behind and strike up a conversation with Soli. "Want to tell me more about the book?" I ask her.

"Oh, you'll like this!" she exclaims. "There are these magical creatures from the sea—Korrigans—that help her build a huge wall around the city to protect it from the waves."

"Sounds like good television material."

Soli smiles wistfully. "I know I could do with a few Korrigans around the office."

I snort dutifully but still feel weighed down by the undefined emotions swirling in my gut. Rather than distracting me, somehow Soli's novel seems to be tied into it all. I know that Soli is hoping to come out of this trip with a proposal for her Dahut piece and perhaps something educational on shamanism, as well. What occurs to me is that her spirit is taking her on a much deeper journey—one that will leave her in a different world. I haven't told her all about the vision I had at the stone circle. I don't know quite what to make of it yet, and it feels like telling her would just make her close her inner doorways more tightly—which would ultimately make the transitions that much more painful and explosive. I sigh deeply and Soli looks up expectantly.

"What is it?" she asks.

I say the first thing that comes to mind. "They had us detour there. I think you had your nose in your book already. The sign said we are headed for someplace called Quiberon." Soli lets out an exasperated "nnnnng!" and rummages for the map.

"Don't worry," I assure her. "It's a perfect example of synchronicity. So it will take us where we need to go—right?"

"I hate it when people say things like that," Soli retorts, giving up her search. "It's like letting yourself be carried along like a log in a flooded river."

I wince. Actually, I'm not fond of the idea that "whatever happens is what's supposed to happen" either. However, my ego bobs to the surface with a ready answer. "Not at all. We have the idea in the West that 'going with the flow' means that you just kick back and wait for something to happen to you. Actually it just means being yourself—allowing your true nature to show itself through your actions."

Soli is more interested now. "But how do you know if it's your true nature?"

"Ah—that's the trick, isn't it?" I grin half-heartedly.

Deepening

Alright then—how do you know what your true nature is? And how do you determine if that true nature allows you to be a shaman? Is there a test you can take that tells you that, "if you have more than 120 points in column B, you could be a shaman?" Not hardly. I have worked as an art director, a bartender, a grill cook, and in a variety of other positions, none of which was remotely fulfilling. I never suspected I would one day be communicating with the spirit world on behalf of others.

When I was a child, I had no idea what I would be when I grew up. There were no 'shamans' in my world, and I certainly would have had no desire to become one. It wasn't until much later that I read about shamanism as it shows up in other cultures. Then I was able to look back and recognize that many of the experiences of my childhood—experiences that left me emotionally battered and bruised—were actually preparing me for the role of shaman. It was not so different from the sort of thing that someone in a tribal society might live through that would lead to their being recognized as a potential shaman. It usually comes down to early life trauma, sometimes in the form of deadly illness or injury that the person manages to survive, sometimes in the form of multiple traumas and family deaths. Either of these tend to transform the consciousness of the child, which in some way gives them the capacity to begin training as a shaman.

It is hard enough, even in a pre-technological setting, to recognize when one is called to shamanize. It's a whole lot more difficult when you grow up in a culture that doesn't acknowledge shamanism as a valid job description, or even validate the very senses the shaman uses to accomplish their work.

In a tribal culture, there is a complex myth structure that tells the people how they came into the world they see around them; what their ancestors did when they got here; and what their place is in this world. The myths include the larger world of the shaman, and the shaman is responsible for maintaining those stories and for passing them on—making sure that they survive, so that the people survive.

Our post-tribal culture has none of this rich underpinning of myth —at least, not once we enter adulthood. Our stories are disconnected propaganda, with little real meaning for our daily lives.

When someone begins the process of becoming a shaman in a tribal society, those around them probably feel sorry for them—no one would really want to be a shaman, after all—but they recognize it for what it is and accept it. They have a place for the shaman in these societies, even if it is usually on the fringes or even just outside of the village. They see the shaman as the one who walks between the worlds and is thus able to intercede for them with the spirits of these other worlds. It is this very independent nature, in a culture that is founded on the interconnectedness of all its members, that makes the shaman's job as unwanted as it is revered. For people who want nothing more than to live a life as much like their grandparent's as possible, the idea of being picked out of the whole of the tribe to stand outside and speak with the spirits is not exactly enticing.

When someone begins this process of exploring their own nature in our society, they often wind up in the psych ward. They have no context for the experiences that they are going through, and the people around them have even less to go on. Often, when the spirits have decided that a person could be of service to them, they begin creating opportunities for that person to awaken deeper parts of their soul. These opportunities generally look a lot like life threatening illness, loss, trauma—sometimes referred to as the shaman's wounding. It is this deep wounding that catches the attention of the soul and brings it closer to the surface.

For someone who's idea of soul is that of something that goes to heaven or hell when you die, there's not a lot of room for this deep part of your Self to wake up and start talking to you. For people without enough ego strength, it can be enough to make them truly insane. So—generally—the spirits pick on those who at least have a chance of surviving the process with their sanity intact.

For those few who do manage to make it through, the real work begins with the realization that the world is a much bigger place than they were taught in school. What follows is generally a series of initiations that awaken the person's capacity to interact with spirits, travel in the otherworld, heal people, and the like.

These initiations can be completely different from one person to the next, but they all have common themes, because they are introducing common mysteries. That is one way of looking at initiation: An introduction to a mystery—something that is not able to be defined or limited to rational explanation and yet is a meaningful part of our existence. Some of these initiations are very organic and happen simply because it's time for them to happen; the soul is ready and the spirits create an opportunity.

Other initiations can be planned and offered in a less haphazard manner. Planned or ritual initiations can come in a number of ways. For instance, when the person has had enough experience to know when the inner pressure is building, they might choose to go out into nature and make themselves available to the spirits by fasting, drumming, dancing or some other means of altering their consciousness. They might then receive a vision or some other experience that moves them along their path.

Ritual initiations can also be found in various societies—from Native American to Australian aboriginal—that offer initiation into specific mysteries in a safe and sequential manner.

My own initiations have been a rollicking mixture of planned and unplanned. From sweat lodges that turned out to be more than I had bargained for to elaborate vision quests—with no vision—they have each taken me further along the path of becoming...me.

This can all be confusing. It's not as if you pass through a doorway and suddenly you are shaman. It is a process—a long and complicated one. These initiations build your awareness, deepen your capacity, hone your skills, so that you can serve in the role of shaman more effectively.

There is a tendency in our Western culture to believe that we are the masters of our own destiny. This leads us to think that we could never be driven to take on a role that we don't chose of our own free will. But trying to avoid taking on the role of a shaman, once the spirits have chosen you, is a recipe for disaster. They will persist until there is not enough left of you for them to bother with. And the thing is, if they have chosen you, it's because your soul wants what they have to offer. It's only our egos that want to believe otherwise.

Chapter 7
Les Korrigans

We continue to follow the signs for Quiberon, letting go of the idea of seeing Carnac, and now I feel myself getting excited. The road takes us onto a peninsula, along a winding road through rocky hills with glimpses of the ocean glittering in the brilliant sun from numerous inlets. At one point the water draws in on both sides, until we are driving across little more than an earthen bridge, and then we are climbing into rocky hills again.

We pass through several villages, one after another, and I have a growing sense of anticipation—though I've no idea what is coming. We stop at a village church, built—no doubt—on the ruins of a pagan temple. We scour the small graveyard for signs of what may lie ahead of us, and come away with no further clues. Back at the car, Soli takes the wheel again, keeping her eyes peeled for our next encounter with synchronicity.

I shade my eyes against the brilliant sun. It is only just before noon and we have parked in a small public lot, squeezed in between angular white houses and an overgrown garden, somewhere in the village of Saint-Pierre-Quiberon. The streets here seem to run in slanted spirals like an Escher print come to life, through a maze of narrow twists and turns. Beneath the knot of the village the earth energy follows a straight path, cutting directly through the tangled pattern of buildings, streets, plumbing and flower boxes. This odd juxtaposition of spirals and straight lines grabs my attention and reminds me that I've been following this pattern of ley lines in my Medicine Body all along the length of the peninsula.

I realize that I'm staring off into space and notice that Soli has already popped out of the car, crossed the street and is waiting for me there. She is smiling and waving for me to come over.

"Yes?"

"Don't you see?" She nods to the signs on the building behind her.

"See what?"

"The Korrigans. Those are the sea creatures from the myth, from the Ys story—the one in my book! The ones that helped Dahut build the dike around her city. I saw a sign on the way into the village and I knew we had to stop here," she explains.

"Ah!" So—more synchronicity. "I guess we should eat our lunch with the sea gnomes then." I open the door and we go inside. The interior is cooler and crowded with faces bearing similar features. The same hair, the same brow, and the same... Soli chuckles and whispers to me.

"I suspect the famous Bretonic nose is inherited from the sea gnomes. What do you think?"

We take the one small table open and place an order from the busy waitress, who seems to be the only one not from this neighborhood. Surrounded by a latticework of conversations from the various workers eating their lunches in the crowded dining room, we sit quietly for several minutes. I let my senses move into the earth beneath us and a bit back toward the center of town, tracing the bundle of ley lines that has been tugging at my awareness.

I'm startled when Soli touches my hand and I look up to see the waitress waiting for me to move my hands so she can set down my plate.

"Where were you?" Soli asks as the waitress leaves.

"Downstairs—in the earth." I reply, smiling. "There's a strong flow of earth energy that's been pretty much paralleling our drive down the peninsula all morning."

Soli's smile slowly blossoms and snorts. "Now I know you're putting one over on me. You were probably just wool gathering."

"No. I'm serious." I lean forward, intent on convincing Soli of my sincerity. "It was nagging at me on the way here, and I just realized what it was after you started driving about an hour ago.

"Since when?" Soli responds.

Thinking back, I remember the thick blood stain on the road. "Since we took the detour around that accident."

Soli stares at me, as if to determine if I am teasing her or not, then slowly shakes her head. "I never know if what you're saying is really happening—or if you're just making it up. At least I know that I can't feel those things."

"Don't be so sure," I reply. "You pick up on a lot more than you give yourself credit for. Remember that couple in Cambrai? The ones you booked a room for to keep the woman from hooking up with her old boyfriend just as he's getting married? That was pretty impressive."

Soli practically explodes with indignation, "Oh, come on now! I just made that up. I don't know anything about those people." Her face is red now and she grasps her fork as if she will have to defend herself with force.

Smiling, I reply, "Perhaps. But your explanation sure seemed to fit their actions. How do you explain that?"

"Hrmph! Producer's instincts!" Soli insists.

Laughing, I turn back to my meal. It doesn't feel like she's ready to be pushed on this.

Soli is not ready to drop the subject entirely though. "That earth energy you talk about. How does that work?"

Grasping this as a perfect opportunity to play with my food and use my degree in Fine Arts, I create a visual model for her. Lining up several carrot sticks on my plate, I cover them with a layer of mashed potatoes, while Soli watches—perplexed. "You see—the carrots are the ley lines, like underground powerlines, that allow the natural energies of the earth to flow from one place to another."

"Why?"

"Because the earth is like a big body—and just like us, it needs nourishment. If one of these lines gets blocked or broken," I nudge one of the hidden carrots out of line. "The energy gets backed up and dissipates. For the lines to work, they have to be open and connected, which allows the energies to flow naturally. Just like the energy does in your body."

"How do you feel this energy…I mean, what does it feel like to you?"

Thinking for a moment, I let myself feel the earth's energy again, pulsing beneath us. "It's kind of like feeling the blood flow through a person's arm—only bigger. Why?"

Soli seems just a little bit troubled. "It's really nothing, but—it's like the 'dragon lines' in the Ys story."

"Ys?"

"That's the city that Dahut is building in the book. To give it power, she gathers the dragon lines beneath the earth and makes them flow down the peninsula to where she builds her city. Can you really do that?" I feel the hair raising on the back of my neck.

"I honestly don't know." I shrug. "There are some who think it's possible, but I've never seen it done."

Soli's eyes focus inward and she finishes the rest of her meal in silence. We pay the check and return to the car.

Deepening

"There is only one center—it just happens to be everywhere." This is Grandfather's favorite answer to most of my questions. He seems to enjoy a zen approach.

I first met Grandfather years ago, when I was still not sure what sort of path I was on, long before I officially became a shaman. He was first just an undefined presence that showed up when I would meditate. Gradually he took on the shape of an old Native American man with long, gray-white hair. As I recall, he spent the first several years of our relationship just laughing at me. He would make suggestions. I would ignore them. I would wind up doing something stupid instead, and he would laugh at me. It got to be rather predictable. Meanwhile, when I did occasionally ask him questions, he'd just say, "You already know the answer." To my question, "Who are you?" he simply responded with laughter. Everything was hilarious to him. Often, he'd say, "Have you noticed such and such…?" pointing out obvious details that I had, of course, completely missed. Over time, I began to realize that when I listened to him, good things would happen. Eventually I just got used to him, and it came as a surprise to me when I realized that we had developed a friendship and that I was actually listening to him and learning from him.

We talk often but our conversations are usually circular, not unlike the following where he explains the one center:

Me: "How does it all work?"

Grandfather: "There is only one center…."

Me: "Where do I get my energy from?"

Grandfather: "There is only one center…."

Me: "How do I enter this world at birth?"

Grandfather: "There is only one center…."

It took me more than a few years to actually start hearing what that meant. That there really is only one center—that it really is everywhere. That every whole being has a center, and that center is every other center—a great spinning spiral. This center lies at the heart of every star, every tree, every person, every stone. It is the heart that ties us together. It is the door that leads to both the inner and outer worlds, the door to infinite possibilities. It is the eye of the god/dess, and it exists within your own body.

When we enter our own inner worlds, we move through this center; our clearest path through it as humans is through the heart chakra. Just as your physical body surrounds the outer world center, your inner body surrounds the inner world center, but of course, these centers are one.

As difficult as it has been for me to realize this Mystery and to put it into practice, it will be relatively easier for the next generation of post-tribal shamans, and easier still for those coming after. Once someone has found their way to the center, it gets easier for the next person to find. Once the door has been opened, it becomes easier to open for everyone.

It's not as if this were a new thing. This center; this doorway, has always been here. However, we super modern, post-technological types have gotten so far away from it that we've forgotten who we are. We've forgotten that there is more to us than the meat and bone of our physical self, and the words and games of our thinking self. So, we go back to this center to remember who we are, to realize what it means to be human in a deeper sense than we learn in the everyday world.

You have already experienced the center, when you practiced the exercise of going into your inner self, through the doorway at your center. That doorway is the center which is everywhere.

Chapter 8
Dragon Lines

The sun is bright on the water as we slowly round curve after rocky curve. Soli is driving now, watching the road intently and perhaps still thinking about our talk on dragon lines and the city of Ys.

The driving has taken on that rhythmic quality again. My body gently rocking against the seat as we curve to the right—now to the left—now to the right again. Speeding up, then slowing, then accelerating once again. Drowsy from lunch and from the warmth of the sun, I am almost asleep when Soli speaks up.

"It's very weird to me—how much this landscape we're driving through reminds me of what I'm reading about in my book."

"Does it?" I ask innocently.

"It's probably just good research on the part of the author. After all, it's supposed to be drawn on an ancient Celtic legend—and they certainly did live around here." She sighs, seemingly comforted by this thought. "There was probably even a city at the end of this peninsula, surrounded by a wall to protect it from the storms at sea. Still, it feels kind of—spooky." Soli laugh nervously. "Strange coincidence, isn't it?"

"Coincidence? Not more synchronicity?" I ask.

"Aha!—Now I remember where I heard that word before." Soli responds triumphantly. "I read about it in Carl Jung's introduction to the I Ching. Hold on—let me see if I remember." We drive on for a bit before she continues. "The theory is that, since every particle eventually comes into contact with every other particle—at some point within infinity—these particles are linked together and can affect one another—right?"

"That's the theory..." I reply. "But how would you apply that to us being here now?"

"Oh—hmmm. . . ."

Silence for another minute, and then: "The particles in the 'Ys' book, and the particles in you and me, and the particles in the land here are all linked because we were all together once—or will be— and so...nnnnggggg!!! I don't get it! What is the connection?"

I have to laugh, "Okay—slow down a bit first. There's more to it than the fact that everything is connected. That's just the given. Because everything is connected, we can sometimes get information, or find ourselves going in certain directions, that have a deeper meaning to them than we can see at first. Synchronicity is what happens when those deeper meanings begin to reveal themselves. Thus the omens of the shaman."

Soli is hesitant to accept this. "Okay—so what deeper meaning is being revealed here?"

I shrug. "We don't really know yet, but we have noticed that the pattern in the book you're reading and the pattern in the landscape we're driving through here are connected. That gives us a clue. Now if you look back to how we got here..."

"But how does that help?" Soli interrupts. "We didn't even decide to come this way. If it hadn't been for that accident..."

"Exactly! The accident." I pause for a moment before continuing. "There is an old tradition that the gates between worlds could be opened with a blood sacrifice."

Slowly it dawns on her. "A blood...you mean that poor person back there—that's disgusting!" Soli's face is red now and she seems confused and on the verge of tears. I think I've pushed a bit fast. Fortunately her mobile phone begins to chirp. Coincidence?

Soli answers the phone one-handed. "Hier ist Soli..." The voice on the other end launches into a long explanation of something to which she replies negatively—several times. By the time she hangs up, our previous conversation seems to be forgotten.

Soli is quiet again, and I am curious myself about what is going on with this journey.

I want to ask her who it was on the other end, but, strangely, don't feel I have a right; it's an interesting quirk of shamanism that you may glance into someone's soul, even live, momentarily, inside their body, but you feel you're crossing boundaries if you ask who is on the other end of a phone call.

Still I am curious about this journey, particularly the ley lines we've been following all morning. To investigate, I decide to slip into shamanic body. "I'm going to close my eyes for a bit –okay?"

"Mmm," Soli replies.

I close my eyes and settle back into my seat. Dropping my attention into my heart center, I open the doorway and move through into my internal space. From here I create a mirror doorway and move through this as well—feeling the peculiar sense of turning inside—out as I pass though the mirror, then into the heart center of my shamanic body and out into that outer body. Then, still in my shamanic body, I step back through the mirror and into the car—sitting down in my own lap for a moment before diving into the earth.

There is a momentary disorientation as I go from the moving car to underground, like splashing into an ice cold lake from a rushing train, then I 'swim' deeper and to the right, following the distant thrum of the ley lines.

I draw closer quickly, suddenly swimming beside them—great throbbing serpents of bright amber and blue and gold light. As I look more closely, I can see the strain and the darker bands of charred black that tie them together. Instinctively I sense that something is not right here. I fly along the pulsing cables, much faster than the car above me. Some miles later, the lines begin to bunch and fray—and there seems to be a double pulse—as if the current is striking a block and washing backwards from the obstacle. The energy is denser and darker as well. It begins to feel hot and swollen, like a wounded limb.

Slowing down now, I am approaching a chaotic tangle of congealed and stagnant energies, beyond which the lines are broken and only a seeping condensation of earth qi continues. I can't think of anything I can do here. It feels too big and too broken.

I let go and let myself snap back toward the car, then flow back through the mirror, through my center and out into my physical body—taking a moment to let my head stop spinning before opening my eyes.

"Have a nice nap?" Soli asks somewhat bitterly.

Given the change in Soli's mood, I wonder if the experience didn't have something to do with her. "I was exploring," I explain.

"That's nice," she replies.

Clearly, the energy has shifted. I notice that Soli's hands are tight on the steering wheel, and her eyes are hooded.

"What's wrong?"

"Where do you get it?"

"Where do I get what?" I say softly, trying to understand the new energy bristling between us.

"Where do you get your—I don't know—power?"

There is silence from my end. It feels like she's angry at me, but with a hint of something else. Jealousy?

"Is it some kind of blood sacrifice like we saw on the road? Is that what it takes to read people's minds like you do, dive into their bodies and shake things up, and go on little mini—breaks to the underworld while other people drive or sleep?"

I take a deep breathe and let it out slowly. "It's not about power," I say. "And the only sacrifice involved is my own."

"Isn't it? Wouldn't we all like to control our realities—to move things with our minds, travel back in time, and hop into other people's bodies?" she asks sarcastically.

I breathe deeply. "Shamans don't necessarily control any more than anyone else," I say firmly. "It's like learning to surf. There are some things you can control and get really good at controlling with practice, like on a surf board. But there are other things that you can't begin to control. Try to control the wave, and you wind up all wet…" I pause. "Shamanism is not about getting what you want. It's not like our disappointing Mystery School seminar that revolved around making what you want magically come to you; it's not like New Age 'magical thinking'; rather, it's about working with what is already there."

There is silence for at least fifteen minutes, possibly a new record for us.

"I'm upset, Kenn"

"I noticed."

"I feel cheated, somehow—like I didn't get to do it."

"Get to do what?"

"Whatever you did at the circle, when you did your diving into the underworld thing that you do…I should have been there. You took my place. Why did you do that? Why did you take on my mission? My karma? What gave you the right to steal my soul's journey?"

I had not thought of it this way, and so I do not respond. In fact, we drive on in silence for several minutes. But I'm not overjoyed and comforted by the peace, as I would have been before; the pause in what had become a steady stream of questions from Soli.

It is Soli who breaks the silence again.

"I'm sorry…that was inappropriate; I just feel like you're doing things to me that I'm not ready for."

"Is that it?" I ask.

"Partly."

I wait before speaking. "Maybe part of why you're upset is my fault—sometimes, I get information that you might not have, and I don't pass it on right away. But that's generally because it doesn't feel like you're ready to hear it."

Soli is silent. "I think what bothers me is that you have access to parts of myself…you're connected to parts…that I'm not able to even feel. But they're me."

I wait for more, but nothing comes, so I start talking. "You will become connected to those parts. It's all part of your journey; that's why we're here. Eventually, you'll have the same access to yourself…to everything…that I do…which is probably why you're so impatient with the process. Part of you knows where you're headed and want's to be there already."

She's silent for a few minutes, pondering the idea. I'm not sure she believes me, but shortly her humor returns. "Well, let's just hope it requires no more of a blood sacrifice than a minor hangnail…" Her abrupt change in mood feels somewhat false, but I'm relieved that the pressure has eased—at least for the moment.

"Well, I think your synchronicity theory is shot," she continues. "If this was the same place as the story, we would have come to Dahut's father's city by now. It was a hilltop fortress sitting astride the peninsula—hard to miss. Instead we are almost to the end. . . ."

As Soli speaks, we come around a particularly slow bend and a large village is spread out below us. Soli pulls the car over and we get out. There may have been a sea wall at some time in the past. There may have been a great stone fortress that we missed on the way here. But the sleepy fishing village at the end of the peninsula looks anything but mythological.

We get back in the car and I drive now, taking us down into the village and along the bay. I see some cafes and ask Soli if she'd like to stop for tea. She doesn't answer and we drive on.

Deepening

Most people—those who at least have some idea of what a shaman is—associate shamanism with mysterious powers. Actually, its more like a set of skills or abilities. For instance, the ability to move into and out of shamanic states of consciousness at will; the ability to move into and out of Shamanic Body or Dream Body; the ability to extend your medicine body into the space around you; the ability to sense the energetic, emotional and psychological state of another person; the list goes on. But none of these "powers" would sound all that impressive on a late night talk show.

The abilities arise from practice and experience. The fundamentals of some of them can be taught. I do this myself in workshop settings. However, it is only with practice that they truly become effective tools in the shaman's toolkit.

One of my favorite things to do when I encounter another shaman is something we often refer to as "swapping shaman tricks." It's really just sharing our maps and the techniques we use for navigating beyond the maps. Generally, we find that we have more in common than not, though we might use different words to express what we are doing.

A case in point is the technique or tool I call Medicine Body. I've run into virtually the same thing with other names used by a

Peruvian-trained shaman and a Tibetan Bon shaman. Like most shamanic techniques, this one makes use of what is already there. In this case, the human energy field. In Chinese Wu shamanism, this field is called the Wei Qi, and it is shown as having three distinct layers. The one closest to the body is described as the physical layer and is closely associated with the physical body itself. The next one out is the emotional layer. The one beyond that is the spiritual layer. Generally this energetic field acts to contain your energies and keep out disease. In this respect, it's rather like an extra, very thick, layer of skin.

In order to go from this naturally occurring energy field to what I call the Medicine Body, we need to increase the quality and quantity of energy in the field to the point that it will support your consciousness. The breathing technique for doing this shows up, essentially the same, in Tibet and in Peru. The technique sounds rather complex—and it helps to have someone lead you through it —but it is basically a series of quick bellows breaths to activate the internal Qi and then an opening of the middle burner/chest cavity and a strong mental focus to draw the Qi upward, eventually bringing it out of the top of the head and into surrounding WeiQi/energy field.

This works because it uses the body's own process of digesting the Qi/energy it takes from the food we eat and the air we breath. This energy is brought into the lower burner/dantien, which is about three inches below the navel. Here it is stored and processed into a form that the body can use for it's own needs. Some of this energy is then drawn up into the middle burner/dantien, located in the heart center of the chest, where it is further digested into what the Chinese call shen, a form of energy which is capable of directing the various process of the body. Finally, some of this energy is drawn up into the upper burner/dantien where it is further digested and then emerges as the WeiQi.

A shaman can build up the shen in his WeiQi to the point that he can extend his kinesthetic awareness beyond his skin and into the energy field that surrounds him. This extended awareness can then be used in a number of beneficial ways for those he is treating. Through the Medicine Body, the shaman is able to extend awareness into the space around his or her own body and that of the client. They are able to sense the flow and quality of the client's energy, more easily detecting, and treating, any blockages or imbalances.

While not a "super hero power," the Medicine Body is a powerful tool for the shaman's work, and just one of many ways to extend consciousness beyond our physical awareness.

Chapter 9
Dreaming on the Beach

It is late afternoon and we have left the Quiberon peninsula far behind and driven on up the coast. We are traveling along a narrow isthmus called Cornuaille. The coast to the one side is fairly calm while the other is wild, and appropriately called the côte savage. We drive off the motorway and up into the dunes and ruins on the côte savage to take a break. We get out of the car and stand for awhile looking over the water, while the wind scours our faces. We don't bother to try to talk. The wind seems to carry all sound in itself already. Anything else would be meaningless.

Returning to the car, we drive back to the motorway and take the next exit to the other coast. Here the breeze is calm and only slightly cool. The beach is layered with dark gravel and pale sand. We stop again, lock the car and walk together on the beach. We are in a good mood, and we've been silent for almost an hour now. As we meander along the beach now, I feel a sense of well—being and "rightness." It feels as if we have caught up to where we need to be and all is well. I don't begin to understand how or why this is so, but the feeling is there nonetheless, so I just enjoy it.

"If you were to have children, what would you name them?" Soli suddenly asks. I look over to her. She has taken me completely by surprise and I'm not sure how to answer. I wonder if this is another of her loaded questions—if there is something more to it than it seems.

"I used to think I would name a daughter Emily," I reply. "But that was years ago. I don't think I would anymore. And I really don't know what I'd name a boy. Perhaps Jonathan, after my older brother—but I doubt it."

Soli smiles. "I used to have a long list of names for babies that I would suggest to my friends when they were looking for names for their children. I think that by the time I get around to having any children myself, the names will all be used up."

"Can't you use the same name someone else does?"

"I don't know why, but that feels wrong." She is frowning slightly. I suspect this is the face she makes when trying to put the last few pieces of a puzzle together. "It feels like those names already have a different meaning for me now and it would be wrong to try to fit a new one to them. I think it's the same reason I don't like it when the names of people I know show up in the scripts I produce."

We continue our walk in silence, finding our way down to a lower level of the beach, where there are high sand bars interspersed with small tidal pools. A flock of seagulls chatter up off the sand as I return to our conversation. "I remember a name that I've always liked—Tamara."

"Yes." Soli nods her head, looking very serious, as if we were considering the name for an actual unborn child. "I like that one too. It means date palm."

"Does it?"

Soli frowns. Her mind has obviously hurried off in another direction—again. Before I can ask her what she's thinking of now, she turns to me and asks: "So how do I do it? How do I get to feel what it's like to go on those...journeys that you take?"

I laugh in surprise. "You might have signaled a left turn there!"

"What do you mean?" she asks.

"You go from talking about baby names in one breath to asking about shamanic journeying in the next."

After a few more steps she continues, "Is that a problem?"

"No—no, just give me a moment to catch up, will you?"

"Okay!" she smiles mischievously. "I'll be good and wait for you."

"Hmmph! Thanks for that." I feel my comfortable sense of everything feeling 'right' beginning to fray a bit. "So why all this interest in shamanism—or are you just making polite conversation?"

"Well—I've been thinking seriously about doing a piece on shamans, and I feel like I need to know something of what it's really like from the inside—or I'll just be another skeptic talking about 'native healers'. If I go to all the trouble of making this happen, I want it to be more than that."

I'm a little startled. "Is this the same project you were working on when we met?"

"No—that New Age piece was an assignment from the station. This is a personal thing. I feel like it is something that people need to hear about." She smiles. "So are you avoiding my question?"

I sigh dramatically. I was in such a good mood and this feels entirely too much like work…."Alright—let's give it a shot." Smiling, I sit down on the gravely beach and motion for her to join me. She does so, smiling expectantly. I move part of my awareness out into my Medicine Body, so that I can feel her more clearly and know how to proceed.

"It all starts with stillness. That's the doorway into the other places that I go to. If you want to try it, just close your eyes." Soli obediently drops her eyelids closed. "Now relax your muscles and let go of your thoughts." She shifts a bit to get comfortable and her facial muscles begin to relax. I extend my Medicine Body around her and can feel the energetic agitation in her head that tells me that she's still in her thoughts.

"This is not about 'getting it right,'" I tell her. "It is not a test. So, let yourself come down out of your head and into your center. Somewhere around your heart." I wait until I can feel her focus drop down. "That's it. Now just listen to the sound of my voice. How it comes out of nowhere . . . moves through you . . . And disappears." Her face relaxes even more, and I gradually lower the pitch of my voice as I speak, drawing her down with it. "Now let your thoughts do the same thing. Don't try to repress them—that will just make you more agitated. Let them arise . . . let them pass through you. . . and let them go. You just keep your focus in your center, and as thoughts arise, you acknowledge them and let them go . . . while you remain in your center. . . ." Her breathing is beginning to deepen now and I can feel her dropping into a quieter state. I reach out with my own energy through my Medicine Body to support her and help her to feel secure in this new territory called Stillness.

"Keep focused," I say softly as she begins to drift off center. "Just acknowledge the thoughts—and let them go." I let her take awhile to become more comfortable with this stage, allowing the surges of thoughts and sensations to begin dropping off; then I continue. "Now turn you attention inward. Move deeper into your center— deeper still. There is a doorway at this center. It is right in front of you. Let yourself reach out and open the door. . . Feel the flow of light and energy as it opens." Soli's face relaxes even more now as her breathing drops deeper and slows. It's as if her whole body is connecting into itself more fully.

"Simply feel the flow emerging though this opening and let it fill your body, while you stay focused here in the doorway." Through my Medicine Body, it feels like her focus has become absolutely centered into that doorway and at the same time, has opened out into her whole body.

We sit like this for a few more minutes, with sporadic reminders to keep her centered, and then I begin to bring her back up. "Feel that current emerging through the open door. Allow yourself to be carried slowly and gently outward by the current until you fill your whole body." Gradually expanding my own energetic cocoon around her, I help Soli come back into her physical body and its ordinary state of consciousness.

After a minute or so, her eyes flicker open. Her face is very relaxed and her eyes seem clearer than before. She smiles and softly breathes, "Wow."

"Does that answer your question?" I ask.

In answer, Soli unfolds her long arms and stretches her fists high over her head, opening her mouth into a powerful yawn. "No. I asked how I could go on journeys, and you just showed me to the doorway. Isn't that right?" I shrug and nod.

"Well, you must know I'm going to want more than that." I continue to nod, smiling knowingly.

"But it will do for now, because right now, I desperately need a nap." That said, she peels off her sweater, rolls it up for a pillow on the dark pebbles of the beach, and settles down for a snooze.

"Okay. I'm going to walk on down the beach. I'll be back." No answer. I draw my Medicine Body back in and stretch a bit myself before getting up and moving down toward the water's edge.

Finding myself suddenly alone, I'm not sure how I feel. I wander on down the beach, stopping to pick up a few colorful shells. It feels like there is more to this action—more to all actions—than I am aware of in the moment, so I am trying to pay attention, believing that I will remember these moments years from now, that they will gradually become laden with meaning as I come to understand more of the journey I am undertaking—more of myself.

Already this road trip is teaching me more about myself. Much of it from watching Soli and finding out more about what makes her tick. As different as I feel she is from me, there are still similarities and many pieces for me to add to the puzzle. I smile, remembering Grandfather once arranging a handful of stones on the floor of his lodge. I ask him what he's doing and he tells me that he's adding pieces to the puzzle. I chew on this for a minute before asking him what it is a puzzle of. He looks up at me innocently and relies, "why, everything, of course."

As I choose the shells, I am aware of a sense of connectivity—as if these colorful tidbits are representative of other larger parts of my world—pieces of the puzzle that is everything. I wonder what pieces these shells will correspond to. There is a purple/black stubby curl of shell that suddenly seems to come into focus, as if some deeper part of me recognizes it. I let go of my thinking mind and, still staring at the shell, I move my focus deeper into my body, connecting into that part of me that is eternal. I feel a deep welling of old pain and I feel compelled to slowly turn the shell, as if it was full of liquid and I was pouring it out onto the sand. The pain slowly eases and the sensation of connectivity fades.

Looking down at the rest of the shells in my hand, I suddenly have a strong hunch that they will be useful later in this journey, and that I should choose them with care, but I take time to toss the purple/black shell, now empty, as far as I can back out into the water.

I don't know how long it takes me to feel that I have collected enough shells. Certainly my pockets are full and I've entered that slightly altered state that is easily found by collecting seashells. And my lower back is stiff and complaining from the constant stooping to capture yet another pretty treasure.

The beach here is covered with rolling dunes and I realize I've left Soli on her own somewhere out of sight up the beach. I feel a little surge of guilt and start to hurry back. It is awkward to run on the sand and gravel, especially since I'm wearing sandals, but instead of slowing out of caution, I pick up speed. I come to the top of a dune, from which I can see Soli, and as I start down the other side, my ankle turns and I almost fall. It doesn't seem to hurt, but doesn't want to take my full weight either.

Soli is still asleep as I limp up to her and lower myself to the gravel beside her. Her body is still, but her face wears a slight frown and subtle tremors pass beneath her skin. I can almost feel her dream body arguing with someone—somewhere.

Suddenly she is awake. Her eyes open, staring up at the darkening sky and then turning to look at me. For just a moment I can feel both her dream body and her physical eyes seeing me, and then the dream presence fades. She looks back into the sky.

"I was dreaming." She begins. "I was at the office, working on a project about the status of education in our society today...something like that. I was waiting for Gebhard and Michael to bring in the films. I could do nothing until they showed up and they were late, so I went looking for them. Somehow I was looking for them at my old boarding school, when I went into a room where an old woman was sitting behind the teacher's desk. She was dressed all in black, like a Spanish matron. She looked at me and her eyes told me to sit down and be quiet. I sat at one of the desks and there was a test there. It was an entrance exam for a state teacher's board. I thought, 'But I don't want to be a teacher.' Instead of filling in the answers on the exam form, even though I know the right answers, I start drawing eyes on the page. While I'm doing this, another woman appears in the desk next to me. She is all dressed in pale green silks and she smiles to me. She is exactly the opposite kind of woman from the dark woman behind the desk. The woman in green motions for me to be quiet and then leads me out of the room. For some reason, the woman in black doesn't seem to notice us leaving. We go through the door into an open meadow and I just feel so relieved to be out of there that I laugh and prance around on the grass. The woman is still smiling, but she tells me that I must take her test now, if I am to stay here and be free. She takes my hand and leads me into a forest. We come to a garden and she has me sit on the ground and places a single seed in my hand. She doesn't say anything, but I know that she wants me to make the seed grow. I try to think of how to explain to her that the world isn't like that. That we can't just do things because we want to. There are responsibilities, expectation. . . jobs to do! I want to do what she asks, but I feel like there's no way that I can, and so I will loose this freedom. But as I sit there, no words come to me and I feel hopeless and lost and start to cry—and then I woke up."

I stand up slowly, lifting myself from the dark pebbles while looking out at the sea as if the meaning of Soli's dream is washing toward me with the foam. I suddenly feel cold and realize it's getting dark. Soli clambers to her feet, shakes out her sweater and pulls in on. I begin to walk back toward the road that runs behind the dunes. Soli notices my limp as she follows me and asks, "What happened to you?"

"I was running on the beach and I think I landed on it wrong." The pain in my foot is a little abated by the cold creeping in from the damp ground and the cooling breeze.

"So, what do you think of my dream?"

I shrug my shoulders. Dreams are rarely as clear to ourselves as they are to others, but I don't want to ruin the realization of the dream for her. "Before I tell you what I get from it, what did it feel like to you?"

"I just felt very anxious. Like I was supposed to know more than I do. That I'm not good enough–or something."

"What if you look at the tests you were offered as two different ways of looking at the world—The first is offered by a stern and dour woman in black, who demands your perfection without offering anything in return. The woman in green begins by offering you freedom and then asks for you to learn and grow in order to stay with her. Perhaps she is offering you a different way to see the world—and yourself. But your old way of looking at the world is in conflict with what she is offering you, and your fears are in the way as well, so you don't realize that you can do what she asks."

"I can?" Startled, Soli stops and looks at me. This question seems to open some vulnerable place within her. She really needs to know. I let myself feel the place in me that knows my answer to be true. Looking into her eyes and willing my words to reach into the part of her that already knows them to be true, I answer.

"You can." We have made it back to the car. Soli looks down at the car keys in her hand.

"So," I ask. "Are your ready to continue our search for the illusive Ys?"

She smiles and unlocks the doors. "Maybe not, but let's get moving anyway. It's getting chilly."

Deepening

When you go through the doorway at your center, you have access to a great many other bodies. We will be exploring some of these bodies later in this book, but for now I want to focus on the Dream Body.

There are—at the very least—two kinds of dreams: The ones that happen inside your own mind, and the ones that happen in the dreamscape beyond. It is similar to the difference between creative visualization and shamanic journeying. With creative visualization, you are moving through images created in your imagination, within the confines of your self. When you move into your Shamanic Body and go for a journey, you are traveling in a different body, through a landscape that exists beyond your imagination.

The dreams you experience while you sleep are much the same. When you have dreams in which you are all the people in the dream, and you are seeing yourself from outside your body, these are inner dreams, dreams inside your own mind. When you have dreams where your perspective is similar to how it would be if you were in your physical body, seeing out of your own eyes and not from an external 'camera view', this is generally an indication that you are outside your internal self. In this case, you are traveling in the outer dreamscape with other dreamers. This is not the only indication, nor is it as simple as I make it sound, but it gives you some idea of the difference.

These dreamscape dreams give you the opportunity to communicate with others in your dreams—and in theirs. Make a note of anyone you meet in this sort of dream. You may encounter them later, or they may already be people you know in your waking life. There are often common settings for these dreams as well, places that you return to frequently. For myself, there is a large outdoor festival field near a wooded area that I visit several times a week. I meet others there to work on ceremonies, dance and drum around the fire together, and sometimes just to socialize. The people I meet there are a mix of ones I know in my waking life and others I know only from meeting them in the dreamworld. Some I see only once. Others I meet there again and again.

It can be easy to enter your Dream Body. There are ways to do it consciously, but most people do it naturally anyway. If you hold clearly and strongly to the intention of moving into your Dream Body before you go to sleep, this can be enough to make it happen. Once again, this is nothing new. We've always had these bodies. We are just not used to being conscious of them or aware of when we are inhabiting them.

One thing to keep in mind is that when you are in your Dream Body, you are in a very different state of consciousness. You may not have the same focus or intention that you had when you went to sleep, and so it's often the case that you might go to sleep with a particular intention—say, visiting a distant friend—only to find yourself distracted by the sensations of the dream and never accomplishing what you set out to do. This is only natural. We are very influenced by the substance of what we take on in our different bodies. This substance is what your Dream Body is made of, just as your physical body is made up of physical matter. Play with this substance. Discover how it works for you. You may notice that it is much more malleable than your physical substance. In your dreams, for instance, you can change your shape, fly, breathe water and do all sorts of things that would be impossible in your waking life. And yet, seeing as how everything is connected, as you learn to manipulate the substance of this dream body, you will find that it has an impact on your waking life as well.

Chapter 10
Hôtel Ys

The drive along the coast is quiet. Both of us have our own thoughts about what we might find, despite the disappointments of yesterday's drive down Quiberon. The sun is warm and golden and Soli seems to be driving more slowly as we round one long curve after another, as if she is putting off arriving at the end of this spit of land.

Soli has me reading to her from her journal, where she has translated sections of the book she's been fixated on, describing the city of white stone in its sheltered bay with Dahut's palace overlooking the city streets, wharves, and pagan temples. But the coast we are passing is rocky and grey, with patches of sickly yellow scrub, revealing nothing of civilization, ancient or modern. Soli seems disappointed—I think some part of her still hopes to finally arrive at the mythical city described in her paperback novel —perhaps on this peninsula, since Quiberon didn't pan out.

Finally, I stop reading and watch as we round the last long curve and look out over the water. We are coming up on a tourist overlook.

"Let's pull over here," I suggest, and Soli guides the car to a stop on the gravel shoulder. We get out and walk to the railing, looking out over the small open bay below. The broad beach curves the width of the bay, eventually disappearing at each end into a jumble of grey boulders which extends out into the bright froth of the sea. Inland from the wide blonde strip of beach, runs a narrower stripe of dark grey, and then the road itself. On the far side of the road are further bands of yellowish green that climb inward and upward. In the center of the road's curve, set along the dark strip of gravel just in from the road, stands a single rambling grey building, surrounded by a black asphalt parking lot, mostly empty. If this was the location of fabled Ys, then it wasn't all that large a place.

I search for some sign of an ancient city here, but can only make out the broken crescent shape of what may have once been a sea wall extending out to encircle the bay.

"Nothing lasts forever, right?" Soli quips with a sickly smile. "It's smaller than I thought it would be. But I guess the palace would have been over there," she says, pointing at the rising steps of green. Then she drops her hand to the railing. "What am I saying? After all, it was only a story."

I smile, and Soli frowns at me. "You find this amusing?" she asks.

I shake my head, still grinning. "It just reminds me of a zen koan. The student comes running up to the master, excited about his realization. He says, 'Master, I see it now! All that we experience— the trees, the mountains, even our bodies—none of it is real! It is all a dream.' Then the student stops and considers. 'But Master, if all of this is a dream, what is real?' The Master turns around and slaps him hard across the face and asks him calmly, 'What hurts?'"

Soli hurumps and pouts, "I don't get it. What is real then?"

By now I know that Soli doesn't have much patience with zen, so I search for some other way to get the point across to her. "We were just talking about dreams a little while ago," I tell her. "It's a bit like that. Actually there's a Tibetan shamanic technique with dreams that can make it pretty clear. Would you like to try?"

She shrugs and turns toward me, settling her hands onto her hips. "What do I need to do now?"

"It's easy! Just let yourself relax for a moment—loosen up."

She sits down on the guardrail and shakes her hands out, then rests them in her lap and closes her eyes. I am impressed with her willingness to continue trying these things when they are obviously really triggering her fears and resistance. She is certainly courageous.

"Okay. Now imagine that you are in a dream. Imagine that you are dreaming that you are sitting here beside the road." A pale yellow Citroen rattles past us and on around the curve, descending into the cove. Soli's eyes come open and follow the car. "Good! Keep your eyes open, and allow the yellow car to be a part of the dream too. The breeze. . . the cry of the sea gulls. . . the red of your dad's car. All of these are a part of the dream."

Now I begin to move into the dream myself, feeling Soli's consciousness beginning to shift deeper. It's as if I'm watching someone going down through a tall building in a glass elevator. I can sense her realizing that she is dreaming. I look around and begin to pick out the pieces of the dream myself. The pea gravel under my shoes. The slightly salty scent to the air. The movement of the waves out to sea. All of it comes together—around us and inside me—creating the sensation of being in a dream.

"Notice that you are not alone in this dream." Soli glances up at me. "That's right. I'm in this dream with you." I smile at her and she smiles back. "We are dreaming this together." As I say the words, I feel my body becoming more sensitive, more sensually aware, more. . . dreamlike. It feels like everything is larger, more colorful and in a strange sort of slow motion. My smile grows as I see that Soli is feeling it too. "Pretty cool, isn't it?" I ask her.

Still smiling broadly, Soli lifts her hands in front of her and slowly caresses the one with the other, her fingertips sliding gently across her palms and then reaching to her face, where she traces the shape of her eyes and then her lips. Her eyes catch the motion of a pair of gulls overhead and she turns to follow them, then suddenly turns back to me, her eyes wide.

"What is happening?" she trembles. "What is this?"

"Don't worry," I tell her. "It's only a dream." I smile, and after a moment, something seems to soften inside her and she begins to laugh.

"It feels so good," she says, still giggling like a schoolgirl. "I feel very . . . straaaaaange!" Soli twists her hands in spirals around her head and rolls her eyes. She explodes in more laughter and I join her. It does feel good. My heart feels more open and light. My whole body feels alive and pleasantly sensitive. And it feels good to be sharing this with Soli as well. She seems more real to me now, as if I have never really seen her until this moment.

As our laughter calms, I look deep into eyes and tell her, "Thank you, Soli."

She actually takes it in, easily and naturally, and after a moment she places her palms together in front of her face and bows slightly toward me, her eyes still joyful.

The afternoon is turning cooler, despite the bright sun, and it is suddenly clear to both of us that this dream should continue in the shelter of the car.

The sound of our doors closing, one after the other, seems to draw us outward from the depths of the dream. The emerging is comfortable though, and necessary.

Turning to Soli, I tell her, "It's best to come back out of the dream before operating heavy machinery. . .."

"Like my Dad's mercedes?" she asks, patting the steering wheel in front of me.

"Yes—very much like that." And we both laugh together again, but the dream is already fading and after a few more minutes of silence it gives way to the ordinary, leaving behind some of the openness and joy in its wake.

"That was very weird," Soli comments. "Were we really in a dream?"

"I can't say. I suppose it depends on what you consider a dream and if there is really anything that's not a dream."

Soli appears to take this in stride and just nods her head as if this makes perfect sense to her now. Perhaps it does. But I know that in this dream, if I run into something, it will hurt. So I bring my attention more fully into my body before starting the engine.

I drive now, taking us down the gently sloping side of the bay, past scrub and dark grey rocks and into the parking lot beside the lone building, which turns out to be a nondescript tourist hotel. It looks to have been built early in the 20th century with weathered wooden clapboard and a long porch that embraces the whole seaward side.

I turn off the engine and we just sit for awhile. The salt is heavy in the air, along with an odor of wet, decaying wood. I know that I don't feel like driving any further. I just want to flop down somewhere and let my brain go off line for a bit, while Soli grieves for whatever was once here—even if it was only a fantasy. I look over at Soli, and she simply nods.

Soli remains silent as we enter the front door and walk to the registration desk, leaving me to muddle through the process of getting us a room for the night. We are shown to a room overlooking the beach, and Soli climbs onto the bed with her journal and the well—thumbed book on the fabled city of Ys, shutting out the rest of the world. I decide that it's time for me to be somewhere else for awhile so I grab a sweater and head out.

The idea of a walk appeals to most of me, but not to my right ankle, which has swollen a bit, so I look for a place to elevate it.

The furniture on the wide porch is weathered but comfortable. I settle into a chair, resting my feet on the wooden railing, and let the tension flow out of my shoulders and back. There is little energy to feel beneath the ground here. Most of it has been dispersed miles back along the road. What remains is the natural qi of ocean meeting land, and the inevitable conversation that results. I close my eyes and lean back to listen, weaving tendrils of qi through my ankle to gently unwind the inflammation and support its healing.

The unexpected squeak of the wooden porch pops my eyes open and I see a tall skinny man slipping into the chair next to mine. He carries a weathered copy of Durant's The Story of Civilization, Vol. IV The Age of Faith, and I find myself wondering if there is any mention of Ys in there.

"Fascinating, isn't it?" the man asks after placing the unopened book on his lap and setting his feet on the railing as well.

"The weather, the sea or the simple beauty of it all?" I ask.

"Ah!," he replies. "I thought you were American. Do you mind if I bend your ear a little? I haven't had a chance to talk to anyone in weeks. My French is just good enough to confuse the locals, and I can't find anyone here to speak English so that I can understand them. I've even started reading any English language books left here by other tourists. Pretty dull stuff," he says, lifting the Durant and dropping it back to his lap.

"So what brings you here?" I ask, feeling how he longs for the chance to talk.

"Well—as I said, this place is fascinating. The peninsula used to continue on out for another few miles, and the land was very fertile. But some few thousand years ago, the end just fell off into the sea. We don't know the cause, and the tectonic plates are extremely stable here—so it's a mystery. Speaking of mysteries, those islands out there…" he says, pointing toward a string of grey lumps on the horizon, "are probably what's left of the old end of the peninsula. There are local legends that they belong to the Devil, and when the Christians built a convent on one of the islands, all the nuns became Satanists."

"I see what you mean by calling it fascinating." I feel an unexpected wave of pleasant warmth roll through me at the realization that Soli's myth does seem to have some place in "reality", and I feel myself more energized now and respond with appreciation and gratitude for how beautifully the universe weaves it all together.

"Oh—that's not even the interesting part," my new companion continues, as if he realizes the impact it's had on me. "What's really fascinating is that there is an almost identical peninsula in Cornwall, complete with a broken tip and left over islands—and similar local tales. It's almost as if it's the same place—in two places...or something like that."

"What are you—a geologist?" I ask.

"No. Geology is only a hobby for me, but I do teach anthropology at Iowa State University. I came across the stories of this place and Cornwall, years ago, and have been wanting to visit ever since. And what is that you do?"

"Ahh—I'm a travel agent—of sorts," I reply, smiling out at the newly awakened stories washing in with the waves.

Deepening

What does it mean to work as a shaman in our post-tribal culture? Among other things, it does mean acting as a travel agent—of sorts. The journeys are in other worlds for the most part, but it's as close a job description as any.

Even in this culture, a shaman still works in service to a community. However, my "community" consists primarily of the loosely connected group of people who come to me for shamanic work. For many, their only connection with one another is that they happen to see me on a regular basis. For some there is a deeper connection, strengthened by participating in workshops and ceremonies together. Unlike the classical tribe however, they have no shared stories, myths or inner maps outside of the work they do with me, to tie them together into a cohesive society.

When a member of the tribe comes to see the shaman in a tribal setting, the shaman already knows a great deal about the inner workings of the individual. The shaman is often the one who has told this person the stories of how their ancestors came to be here. If the person comes with dreams to be interpreted, the shaman knows the language of their unconscious, because it is encoded in the shared stories of the tribe. He knows the landscape that their Dream Body walks, because it is the shared landscape of their ancestors. He need only apply this information in an effective manner.

When a new client shows up at my office, I have to start from scratch. I examine this unknown individual from top to bottom—using my Medicine Body to take in more information than my conscious mind is aware of. It is my responsibility to determine their souls' maps, myths and inner landscapes. Without this understanding, it is difficult to do more than superficial work. Much of the first few sessions is taken up by the process of learning what makes this person tick. The essence of this process is that I move myself into my own soul level of consciousness and from there I observe their soul. This is the level where most of our work will be done. I am not a psychotherapist, so I have no interest in working at a psychological level. In fact, I do what I can to actively discourage my clients from interacting with me in a psychological vein, as this draws them—and me—out of the part of them where we are doing our work together, and lessens the impact of that work.

Once I have a clear idea of the inner dynamic, I can still be constantly surprised by the images that appear in that landscape. This is primarily because the symbolic language of people in our culture is a patchwork of icons borrowed from television, movies, parents, schooling, ancestors and all aspects of popular culture. Unlike people who are raised in a traditional tribal setting, we do not have a clear cultural heritage of our own. This is both a blessing and a curse. On the one hand, it gives us the freedom to look beyond any one "truth" to see a larger world than would otherwise be available to us. On the other hand, it robs us of a sense of cohesion and belonging. It also makes the job of a shaman much more difficult.

This challenge would be more of an obstacle if I were working at a psychological or emotional level with my clients. Instead, my job is to move to a soul level within myself, and to speak to them—from my soul to theirs—with clarity and compassion. This often feels rather like being an open door through which the breeze of the soul sometimes blows. I can find myself saying things in this state that I have no intention of saying, and yet the outcome is almost always positive. It becomes even more interesting when a client asks me a question in this state of consciousness and I listen to the answer coming out of my mouth, while thinking incredulously, "I didn't know that."

Chapter 11
Onward & Inward

We enjoy a light breakfast in the common room of the hotel, planning our day's journey as best we can, allowing for the input of synchronicity. I expect to see the American professor, hoping to introduce him to Soli, but he doesn't appear before we are ready to leave. We pay our bill and carry our bags out to the car. There is a definite sensation of an ending and an impending beginning like intermission at the theater. I smile at the thought that we are responding to the ushers flipping the lights on and off. Time to head back for act II. And it's my turn to drive again.

"So you think that Ys might actually have been on the southern coast of Britain— not in Brittany?" Soli asks. The energy is back in her eyes, and she smiles, radiant as a child, at the thought that the quest for her mysterious city continues.

"I'm honestly not sure what I think about that, but from what the fellow said, there is a big, shiny synchronicity sitting there," I reply, guiding the car through the sinuous curves of the coastal road. "And from what your book says, it isn't absolutely clear where the story takes place, just that they are a Celtic people, at the beginnings of Christian influence. Even if this is where the city of Ys was, I think if we are still following synchronicity—and it looks like Cornwall's our next stop."

Soli has the map out on her lap and is continuing to chart our best route to a ferry that will take us across the English channel.

"So, tell me," I ask. "Did you read some more in your book?"

"I finished it yesterday," she replies, her mouth turning down at the corners.

There is a long silence, and then, "Dahut builds her city, but the Christians didn't like it and they keep after her. They send a spy into the city. She falls in love with him; they become lovers. She trusts him. Then, at a big celebration of the gods, he steals the keys to the gate in the sea wall and opens them, letting the sea in to destroy the city. That's about it." Soli drops her hands into her lap like crumpled leaves and stares out into the bright morning sun. "Just another example of how relationships can screw you up."

Very carefully, I reply, "I can see how it might look that way."

Soli shakes herself loose of her mood and rocks back into her seat, planting the soles of her shoes against the glove box. "Well then— what's the 'shamanic' perspective on relationships?"

"Pretty weird really." I glance over to see her attention drifting inward. "There's a lot of tradition around the idea that you're supposed to be androgynous—balanced between both male and female, you know. So sometimes the shaman will 'mate' with a spirit; sometime they will dress and live like the opposite sex."

Soli looks over at me—all innocence. "So are you really a girl?"

I'm not sure whether to be offended or amused, but a smile creeps out, nonetheless, bringing a sharp laugh from Soli.

"I'm glad you find the subject of my sexuality amusing," I say with mock wounded dignity.

Soli ignores this entirely. She looks over at me again, truly curious now. "I have some friends in Berlin who are always talking about their experiences with tantra and sex magick. Is that part of shamanism too?"

I am momentarily at a loss for words. Once again, Soli has managed to surprise me. I'm beginning to suspect that she does this on purpose. This is certainly not a direction I ever expected our discussions to take. If anything, our interactions have always been rather asexual.

"Well..." I begin. "Of course that is part of shamanism. After all, shamanism is about integrating the whole self, and sex is a big part of that whole."

Soli purses her lips and seems to be considering this. "Yes—but how exactly? My Berliners seem to find it all extremely fascinating."

"I can't speak for your 'Berliners', but in the U.S. there are a lot of people who see tantra and sex magick as an excuse for sex. The fact that they feel that they need an excuse for sex says more about them than their interest in the subject does."

"What do you mean?" Soli asks, her head tilted to the side.

"What I mean is that, if they were already integrated then they wouldn't need an excuse to explore, play, examine or engage in what is already a valid part of who they are—namely their own sexual nature."

"Yes, yes. . . but I get the distinct feeling that you are avoiding the question I actually asked." Glancing over at her, I notice that Soli has just the hint of a smile. So—she is playing with me after all.

"Okay. . . let me think. What can I tell you about the shamanic perspective on sex. . . ?" There is no reason not to just give her what she's asking for, though I suspect she will be a bit disappointed. "The shaman sees sex as a natural part of the whole —you know—Life the Universe and Everything. For the average person it's enough just to keep in touch with that part of their whole self, which seems to be a bit problematic in our Western culture. There is such a mixture of conflicting messages about our sexuality that we wind up repressing and exploiting ourselves at the same time. Small wonder that it's so fascinating. It's our favorite taboo."

"But that's not Tantra or sex magick," Soli interjects.

"No. Most people don't really need Tantra or sex magick. That's for people who want to move outside of the boundaries of everyday life and start messing with the building blocks of existence."

"Mmmm—sounds juicy!" Soli smacks her lips dramatically and I can't help but laugh.

Growing serious again I continue. "It is pretty juicy, but probably not in the way you mean. The people who are serious about using sex as a means of self transformation generally wind up in some scary places."

"Oh come off it!" she retorts. "What's all that scary about sex?"

I resist the urge to ask her the same question, noting that she seems to avoid that whole part of herself. Instead I calmly explain: "Sexual desire is one very clear manifestation of an essential mystery of the universe. It is literally what calls us into Being. When you feel that sense of attraction to another person, you are actually tapping into a huge power source."

Soli is quiet now. I wait a few more beats and then continue.

"Actually, sexual desire is another form of the same instinct that draws us into the journey of our soul's awakening, which is probably the most important part of modern shamanism."

Soli, incredulously, "How do you reckon?"

"Because it is the desire for the other that drives us in both situations. On the one hand it's the desire for some sexually attractive person, and on the other it's the desire for the spiritually attractive soul that we don't yet realize is our own deeper self." I can almost feel Soli's head beginning to hurt. "Take my word for it," I tell her. "It's all connected."

"Hmmph! That still doesn't tell me anything interesting. When you start talking about 'mysteries' my brain just shuts down and stops listening."

"I'm impressed." I tell her.

"What do you mean?"

"Well—I didn't think you had noticed."

Soli takes this in for a moment and then aims a playful smack at my head. I duck and smile before continuing.

"Listen. I know that some of what I'm saying probably isn't making much sense. One of my teachers—one of the ones in this world—told me that if you haven't truly resolved an issue in your own life, it's going to be hard to express it clearly to anyone else. I guess this is just my way of reminding myself that I'm not all that resolved on the whole sexual relationship thing yet. After all, I just got out of a five–year relationship that was sporadically joyful and torturous, and that was probably the healthiest relationship I've had so far." I take a long breath and let it out slowly, trying not to sigh dramatically. "So I guess me trying to tell you about relationships—of any kind—is a case of the blind leading the blind."

"Well! At least the secret is out." Soli grins. "Kenn's not perfect."

"Was there ever a question of that?" Shaking my head, I return to an earlier theme, "So you say you finished your book. Where is it?"

"I left it there," Soli says. "It seemed like a good place to let it go. Almost like I was planting a seed for someone else's adventure."

I smile. "Sounds like you're starting to follow your feelings more."

"Isn't that what you've been telling me I need to do?" Soli replies, smiling now in response.

Deepening

Intuition—what is it really? Is it subliminal perceptions feeding you information at an emotional level? Is it the voice of core values speaking through your likes and dislikes? Is it some inner voice that knows more about the situation than your conscious mind, trying to get you to listen?

Probably all of that is true at one point or another—but it is also a way of describing the input from the sensory apparatus of your various bodies, constantly feeding you information that you don't get through the sensors of your physical body.

Even if you have never developed your Shamanic Body, you still have senses that extend beyond the visible spectrum, and when you realize—sometimes at a pre–or super conscious level—that it is really important for you to be getting certain information, these senses supply it and channel it to your conscious mind. Then it's up to you to find a way of paying attention to it. This process generally results in our feelings of intuition.

Any combat soldier or beat cop will tell you all about following hunches. Sometimes they are the only thing that keeps you from being in the wrong place at the wrong time. The ones who don't follow them don't generally survive the experience. The same can be said of shamans. If they don't pay attention to their intuitive input, then they miss a lot of what they need to be paying attention to, and wind up as rather ineffective.

There's nothing like a life-threatening experience to make these senses kick into gear—or to get you to pay attention to them. I suspect that this is one reason why shamanic initiations are so heavily furnished with scenes of death and dismemberment.

Much of the early work of a shaman is to cultivate their intuition. This is done by going into situations where the intuition is used and tested. One thing that quickly becomes clear is that it is not an infallible guide. No matter how certain a hunch seems to be, only time will prove it, one way or another.

Practice helps us to learn how to differentiate between true intuition and other messages from the self—like wishful thinking, hidden fears or unconscious shadows. Not being able to tell the difference between these varied sources can be a problem—

sometimes a dangerous one. Be careful not to take what appears to be an intuition at face value.

Only practical experience allows you to know, beyond any doubt, when your intuition has given you something golden. Approach the question like a scientist. You are looking for empirical evidence, not justification for your views. Go ahead and try out your hunches, without being attached to the outcome. You are gathering data. Keep a record of when your intuition is right—and when it is off the mark. This record will help you to sense when that quiet voice inside you has something to say that's worth listening to.

Chapter 12
Crossing the Water

The cashier hands me my receipt and change in English coins. Soli and I have been talking non—stop about symbolism and the language of the unconscious since parking the Mercedes in the bowels of the ferry and climbing up here to the cafeteria.

Soli sets her tray opposite mine and takes her seat. I notice she is smiling. In response to my questioning glance, she nods over my shoulder at a gaggle of British school girls, probably returning from holiday on the continent. Looking back at them settling around a group of tables behind us, I see a wonderful opportunity.

"So tell me what you see there." I suggest to Soli, turning back to her at our table.

"I see... A bunch of schoolgirls. What do you mean?" She looks perplexed.

"You smiled when they came in. What did they remind you of?"

"Myself—when I was their age. I went to a convent school—all girls." Smiling again, Soli continues. "We were a rude and evil lot."

"But can you see any familiar types there?"

Soli looks back a the girls again, as if looking for antennae and floppy ears. "It's who they are—how they present themselves."

"Do you mean—like the princess, the bitch and the know-it-all?" Soli asks.

"Something like that."

"Those are the names we had for girls at school. It's weird how easy it is to spot the same 'people' here." Soli nods to each girl in turn, naming their archetype. "She's the misfit who desperately wants to be liked. She's the popular one who walks all over everyone else. She's the 'daddy's girl' who always has a new car..."

"What about her?" I ask, interrupting to indicate a girl sitting at a different table. She is on her own, with a thick book. Her long hair is wrapped loosely in a bun to keep it out of her face and the overall effect is graceful and genuine.

Soli seems stumped, then shifts her gaze to the other table, where some of the popular girls are in a huddle, whispering about something. "They are hatching a plot," she says.

A young waiter is approaching the girls' table and begins refilling the sugar canister. The girls begin to flirt with him, and he blushes, but doesn't respond. Finished with that table, he moves on to the one where the lone girl sits reading. She doesn't notice him at first, and is startled when she does. She is the one who blushes now, as she takes her feet down off the table to give him access to the condiment rack. He mumbles something to which she responds in what sounds to me like quite passable Italian. He smiles and continues in Italian as well.

As the waiter moves on, the girl closes her book, rises gracefully to her feet, and leaves the table. The group at the adjoining table peer after her and immediately break into a storm of whispered conversation. It seems that if they are plotting something, it has to do with this girl.

"Watch this now," Soli warns me. "They will be doing something to hurt her."

"How can you tell?" I ask, curious of just how much she is picking up.

"Because I've been there."

"So—you were the girl with the book?"

She seems uncomfortable with this realization. "I guess so."

"And what archetype is she?" I ask, ever so innocently. In my own mind, I've already named her "Book Girl."

Soli doesn't respond to my question, but instead directs my attention back to the group of schoolgirls. They have called the waiter back over to their table and are leaning toward him and speaking to him in conspiratorial tones. As "Book Girl" reappears with a cup of tea, they shush each other and wave the waiter off.

Suddenly we hear the chirp of Soli's mobile phone. She grabs the phone out of its holster on the strap of her handbag, turns the power off, and sets it aside on the table, still watching the action. I'm frankly amazed. I didn't think she was capable of intentionally missing a call.

The waiter has returned to "Book Girl's" table, glancing nervously at her schoolmates. He bends down and says something to the girl. She looks up at him, startled at first, but quickly regaining her composure. She smiles and responds at length, until, blushing furiously now, the young man turns and hurries out of the cafeteria. It is all Soli can do to suppress her glee, while "Book Girl" nods to the next table, then plants her feet firmly back on the table and returns to her book.

"So" I ask. "Which of that lot do you think would make the best shamanic apprentice?"

"Well—her of course," she says, indicating the girl behind the book. Then, realizing how this reflects on her, she continues, grinning now in spite of herself. "Of course she would also make the best brain surgeon, rocket scientist or—if she's as smart as she looks—even a television producer."

Deepening

One of the things a shaman looks for in his or her work is patterns. We look for repeating images in dreams, patterns of behavior or events, regular cycles of mood or response – all of which give us clues to what is going on with our clients at a deeper level than they are consciously aware of.

For instance, a series of dream fragments in which the client finds herself at a restaurant with no food, finds a loaf of moldy bread and can't find the kitchen in her house all indicate that some part of her is feeling unnourished. By recognizing this underlying pattern I can address the issue more directly and help her to find ways to nourish the hungry parts of her soul.

We also look for patterns in our own experience, behavior and perceptions. These patterns can help us to see into the dark corners where we would normally not be able to look. One way we do this is by recognizing when we are projecting parts of ourselves onto others. These are generally parts of ourselves that we don't see as being us. I will go into this further in a future deepening on shadows. To give you an example: If I have a part of me that is yearning for acceptance and I don't like that feeling, then I don't look at it. I don't see that I have this yearning, so I don't have to feel bad about it. But when I encounter someone else who is yearning for acceptance, all the unacknowledged bad feelings that I have toward that yearning in myself is suddenly aimed at this other person. If I see myself feeling angry or rejecting toward others, for no apparent reason, this is usually a good indication that I am projecting. By realizing this, I can begin to understand what it is I'm putting onto them and then work to take it back.

One way these patterns reveal themselves is through our perceptions. So much of how we see things is influenced by our inner dynamics. What I mean by inner dynamic is the set of internal perceptions and perspectives that make up your sense of who you are. For instance, your response to otherwise neutral elements reveals something about your inner state. If you respond to the color red by interpreting it as passionate, this indicates one thing. If you interpret it as violent, this indicates something else. So the shaman works to be aware of these interpretations and to understand what they reveal.

It might be interesting for you to practice being mindful of your own responses. Notice how you are responding in various situations. How much of your response is based on your interpretation of the situation? What can you learn about your own inner dynamic by this exercise?

Chapter 13
A Walk in the Rain

The rain starts before we even reach the port at Plymouth. By the time our line of cars winds its way out of the embarkation zone, past the "keep to the left" signs, and into the streets of the city, there is a steady downpour.

"I'm sorry. I really don't feel like trying to drive in this," Soli exclaims. I agree, and point to a car park just ahead of us. Soli maneuvers us in between a couple of other parked cars, shuts down the engine and shifts her seat back a bit. We sit silently in the car, watching and listening to the roar of the rain on the roof. I take off my shoe and begin to massage my ankle and foot.

"Is it any better?" Soli asks, noticing my attempt at self healing.

"Not as much as I'd like," I reply. "I'm not used to taking so long to heal."

"Do you think you should see a doctor?"

"No—I don't think someone with a medical degree is going to be able to tell me anything I don't already know about my own body," I snap. Soli doesn't answer, and I can feel her withdraw. "Sorry. I know you're just concerned. It hurts and it's making me irritable."

"I noticed." Soli replies. "Perhaps there's some deeper shamanic meaning to your injury." She smiles.

"You never know. It seems like everything has a deeper meaning these days," I smile back.

The rain stops suddenly, as if a faucet is turned off, and the sun sparkles through the droplets on the windshield.

"I desperately need a walk. . . and, if at all possible, a tea!" Soli says. "Do you think you're up to it?"

We lock the car and walk slowly along the cobbled walks that lead us toward the center of town. I am not exactly limping, but I can tell that my foot would rather be doing something else—preferably something that involves less walking on it. The sidewalks are lined with shops—selling everything from fudge to umbrellas. I am looking into a window, trying to figure out the nature of the crocheted object displayed there, when I almost collide with the woman stepping out of the door.

"Pardon me!" she says as if beeping her horn at me, and stalks off down the walk, snapping her umbrella up and out as she goes. I feel like I've just been sideswiped by a bus. I turn to find Soli, who was looking through a basket of low priced winter gloves, and see her entering the shop.

Following her in, I browse the rack of tour books beside her. "Look at this one," she says excitedly, showing me a postcard entitled "Mystical Lyonesse" over a map of Cornwall. I nod, confused.

"Don't you see? Lyonesse. . .Ys!"

"Isn't that connected with the King Arthur legend somehow?"

"Yes—it's the magickal land that was supposed to be near Cornwall, but got swallowed up by the sea. This is spooky!" But Soli is smiling as she continues to explore the rack.

After some more browsing I interrupt her. "I think I need to find a place to sit," I tell her.

"Time for tea!" she responds. I've learned by now that for Soli, tea time is any time before, between or after any of the major meals of the day, the only exception being that she will generally avoid black tea after five in the afternoon.

Not much later, at Maeve's Tea House, my foot propped up on a chair with a bag of frozen peas nestled atop it, we settle down to scan the stack of tour books, postcards and maps Soli has purchased for her research.

"I wonder what the name 'Cornwall' actually means," Soli ponders. "This is a good question for Len at the office; he does a lot of my research for me." She reaches for her handbag and begins to search for her phone. Her search becomes more and more frantic and she suddenly goes pale.

"What's wrong?" I ask her.

"My Handy—my mobile phone! I left it on the ferry." She looks as if she is in shock at first, but then slowly peers over at me. "This isn't another one of your blasted 'synchronicities' is it?"

"You mean, do I think that leaving your phone behind was an important part of our journey?" I pause to consider this. "Knowing what the phone means to you—all the 'real world' power and the reliance you put on that, instead of on your own innate talents— yes, I'd say it probably is important for you to leave it behind."

Strangely, this answer doesn't seem to help Soli's mood. "I'll have to find a land line to call the office. Let them know where I am!"

"They already know you're on vacation, don't they?"

"Yes, of course!" Soli is clearly exasperated by the whole matter. "But you have to understand, it's not vacation time, so everyone else is hard at work, and I'm sticking out like a. . . lazy thumb!"

"I don't get it? Not vacation time?"

"Civilized people, by which I mean Europeans generally and Germans specifically, have the good sense to take their holidays during the same time of the year, so that everything is organized for that. Not for people taking off on some wild notion—"

"Like us you mean?"

"Yes! Like us and this fool road trip!" She begins stuffing the tour books into her bag and then stops, slamming the purse down on the table, her eyes furious. "I don't know what I was thinking— running off like this! It's completely irresponsible."

"Soli," I say as calmly and quietly as possible. "I'm really sorry about your phone. I know this is really triggering a lot of your issues."

"Issues! I didn't have any issues until I met you! This is all your fault!" Her eyes are tearing a bit and I can almost see the steam shooting out of her ears. "Verdammt schamanische. . . . ." She says nothing for a minute, glaring down at the table. Then she shakes her head, runs her fingers through her short hair and takes a deep breath, letting it out in a long sigh. It's obvious that she is controlling her outburst; packing the rage away for some other time.

She begins again, "No, Kenn. I'm sorry. I'm making this into high drama and it's just a telephone, for Christ's sake. Please don't mind me." Her jaw is still clenched and tight. The words are the right ones, but they are probably not the ones that express what she is feeling right now. Those words are shoved down and stuffed away, and there's nothing I can do or say.

Soli returns her attentions to the remaining maps laid out on the table and we begin to plan our route, but I can tell her heart is not in it.

The rain has started again, lowering the light enough that it is difficult to make out the notations on the surveyor's map I'm exploring, but my eyes keep returning to one point. I can't quite make out the writing, so I tilt it toward the window and finally am able to read aloud: "Boleigh Fogou."

"What's a fogou?" Soli asks.

"I don't know. I don't even know what a 'boleigh' is, but it feels really interesting."

Soli sits there for a moment looking somewhat doubtful before asking, "What do you mean 'feels interesting'? I can't say I've ever felt anything from looking at a map."

"No?" I fold the map and put it aside on the table. "What do you get feelings about?" I ask.

"I get feelings about—general things, I suppose. Going down dark alleys; bad movies; when it's time for tea." She smiles.

"Do you ever sense energy?" Soli looks at me blankly, so I continue. "Here. Hold your hands like this," I say, demonstrating by holding my own hands out over the table, palms facing each other, as if holding an invisible ball. Soli follows my example. "Now pay attention to how it feels as you slowly move your hands

closer together . . . then further apart. Like so," I say—
demonstrating once more.

Soli goes through the motions, not knowing what to expect. As she
slowly moves her hands together and apart, her brows knit and
she says, "That's weird! It's like my hands are magnets." Looking
up at me, she continues, "When I bring them together...it feels like
they want to push apart. But when I draw them apart...it's like
they want to stay together."

"Keep going—it'll be even more interesting in a minute. Now
notice how you're breathing. Take it deeper. Inhale more deeply,
and exhale all the way out . . . now just imagine that you are
sending your breath down through your arms and out through the
palms of your hands. Just imagine," I repeat, as Soli looks up
skeptically.

"Keep going. You're doing great!" I encourage her. "Now as you
breathe in, draw your breath up from the earth and exhale it down
your arms and out your hands." She takes a few deep, slow
breaths and her face begins to relax a bit. Suddenly she breaks into
a smile.

"I can feel it!" She exclaims. "My hands are tingling, and it's like
there's a ball of . . . something in between them."

"That's it!" I agree. "That 'something' between your hands is
energy."

Deepening

Qi—also spelled chi—is a strange thing—at least to the Western mind. It is not just energy, as a lot of people tend to think. It is the substance from which all things, even physical objects and living creatures, are made. It is the stuff of existence before it resolves itself into matter or energy—but it also remains on within form and energy as well.

It helps if you don't try to hold Qi as an idea in your mind, but let go of it—let it be a Mystery. We have few enough of those left in our world, so you may as well enjoy this one.

Qi is constantly circulating through all things and between all things. It emerges from that one center, moves through the world, and returns to that center which is everywhere.

Here is a fairly simple exercise to explore the sense of Qi. Mind you, simple doesn't necessarily mean easy. It will take considerable practice to be able to get much out of it. However, if you are willing to stick with it, this exercise offers you an opportunity to learn a great deal about the nature of Qi.

Find somewhere that you can sit on the ground—preferably outside, but if there's snow on the ground, try your living room. Sit with your spine erect, shoulders relaxed, breathing naturally through your nose, with your tongue resting lightly against the roof of your mouth.

Focus your attention in your heart center and go into stillness. Just sit for a bit. Let go of your thoughts and allow the stillness to take hold. Pay attention to the doorway at your center. Allow it to stand open. You may notice the sensation of a gentle "breeze" passing through. Get close enough to feel the sense of peaceful joy—the cosmic inner smile—that emanates from the open doorway.

As you watch the door, you will notice that there is a constant flow of an energetic substance through the door. This is undifferentiated Qi. That is—Qi that has not yet resolved itself into any particular energy or matter. It comes from the in-between space—the wall between the inner and outer worlds. Its source is infinite, limitless and inexhaustible. However, just because you have a limitless source of energy doesn't mean that using the energy won't wear you out.

Begin following your breath. As you breathe in, draw your attention up the back of your spine toward your head. As you breathe out, drop your attention down the front of your body toward your pelvis. Notice where your attention passes freely and where it seems to either get stopped or skip over places. Wherever you feel a block, imagine a doorway and allow it open wider, until you can feel the energy flowing through smoothly and continuously. Where you feel blank spaces—places where the Qi seems to skip through without engaging—draw your attention into this space and trace the flow of energy through each of these zones until you can feel a continuous movement all the way through them. Proceed in this way until you can feel a continuous flow of energy rising up the back of your body, over the top of your head and down your front. If you feel any blocks that you don't seem to be able to open, discontinue the exercise at once. Building up Qi behind these blocks can be very dangerous to your physical body as well as your emotional and energetic well-being. It can lead to Qi deviations which can result in a variety of symptoms, from chronic headaches and myofascial pain to mood swings and rage attacks. Not something to mess around with.

Continue following your breath up and down, gradually smoothing the flow and extending it, as if you were combing it out, so that each breath takes you all the way down to the bottom of your sacrum and all the way up to the top of your head.

The Chinese call this the Microcosmic orbit. This is a fundamental exercise in the process of connecting with your Qi. If you practice it every day, you will notice gradual positive changes. Your Qi will grow stronger and your awareness of it will increase. Your physical body will come into more balance as well. This orbit regulates and supports the flow of Qi throughout your whole body. When it is open and flowing, the Qi throughout your body tends to be more balanced and healthy.

Chapter 14
Crossing the Tamar

The rain is still making a racket on the roof of the car as we wind our way out of Plymouth and onto the motorway. Soli is driving still and I am trying to find some music on the radio, but all I've found so far is a good selection of cricket and football matches and what sounds like a live broadcast of some government meeting. None of it is stimulating enough to keep us awake.

"Oh look!" Soli exclaims and I glance up to see a wide valley before us, spanned by an attractive modern bridge that looks like a strange sort of insect that has settled over the river to spin its cocoon. As we drive onto the bridge, a rainbow appears over the hills beyond. Soli looks to make sure I see it and we both smile, driving on, sharing this unexpected moment of beauty in silence.

I see by the signs at the end of the bridge that we have just crossed the river Tamar and I notice that it has stopped raining as well, though our wheels still spin up a hissing spray from the rain–darkened pavement. I open my window just a crack and stick the tips of my fingers out to taste the cool, wet breeze. I could feel the shift of land spirits as we crossed over the river, and the new one seems more awake and welcoming to me. Looking over at Soli, I wonder if she has any awareness of this.

"Did you notice the shift as we crossed over that river?" I ask her.

"Why don't you tell me what you mean by 'shift' and I'll let you know if I felt one?" Soli replies with a smile.

I laugh. "Right!" I pull my chilled fingers back into the car and rub my eyes, searching for the right words. I know from experience that Soli is on a powerful threshold. For people who don't include spirits and earth energies in their view of the world, discovering their existence can turn everything upside down. "Okay—It's not all that different from feeling a shift in texture. Imagine that you're running your hand over the dashboard there," I say, pointing at the car's dash in front of her. "In fact, go ahead and do it."

Soli hesitates then reaches out and runs her fingertips over the surface of the console in front of her. She shrugs.

"Okay," I continue. "Now run your fingers on up along the steering column. Feel the shift in texture?"

Soli frowns. "Of course. What's that got to do with what you're talking about?"

"It's basically the same thing," I reply. "The difference is that feeling the shift in the textures of the land we're passing through requires a different set of sensors. You remember that feeling you had in the tea house of 'something' between your hands?"

"Yes," Soli replies cautiously. "But how do I know that wasn't just you putting me into a hypnotic trance and suggesting that I was going to feel what I felt?"

"I suppose you will just have to trust your own senses," I reply. "Do you want me to continue or not?" I really don't know at this point, if Soli is ready or willing to take this further. I can see that this trip is already challenging her world view and her sense of her own identity.

"Go on," Soli says. "I just can't help being skeptical."

"I don't blame you. I'm a skeptic myself. In fact, I think I spent the first ten years or so in this arena trying to prove it was all bullshit

—but back to your question. You remember that feeling when you realized that you could feel something?" I watch Soli as I speak, keeping my attention in my own dantien, as if I had an extra set of eyes below my navel. This is another technique I learned from Grandfather. It's a great help in accessing my intuition, and it seems to be working now. I can sense both Soli's resistance and her excitement at learning to extend her senses beyond what she knew was possible.

"Uh huh," Soli murmurs suspiciously.

"Well—the same sense that was able to feel that 'something' between your hands can be extended to feel a different 'something' out there." I finish, indicating the brilliant green landscape we are moving through. "In this case, it's what I call the land spirit. This spirit gives a particular texture to the land it inhabits, and when you move into the territory of a different spirit, the texture changes."

"Just like that...?" Soli offers.

"Just like that." I consider her wandering gaze for a moment before adding: "Mind you, I think it's a good idea to wait until you're not driving to try it for the first time."

"Nnnnggh! You do this sort of thing all the time while you're driving."

"I'm a trained professional," I reply, a bit smugly. I can feel Soli's mood lifting as she takes another tentative step into a larger world.

"Well! Did Mr. trained, smug, professional notice the most recent synchronicity we just passed through?" Soli half glances at me, her eyebrows lifted inquiringly.

"Ummm—no. I think it's safe to say I missed it. Whatever it was." I admit.

"I'll give you a clue," Soli offers generously. "Remember our discussion of names for children?"

". . .yes. . ."

"And do you not remember the names you came up with?" She actually seems to expect me to be able to figure this one out for myself. I wrack my brain to remember my favorite names. Emily. . .John. . .what was it? Tamara!

"Ah! The river Tamar. It's a variation of Tamara—right?" It's pretty thin as synchronicities go but it does seem to connect.

"Very good." Soli gives me an approving nod. "You have passed this test. You may proceed." We both laugh.

Deepening

I would like to address the topic of spirits in a way that will hopefully be accessible for those raised in the West. As I'm sure is already apparent, we don't really acknowledge the existence of spirits in our Western culture. For the most part, we don't really "believe" such things exist. We have some vague sense that 'something' continues after the body dies, and perhaps we ascribe to the idea that "plants have feelings too." However, we have little experience in recognizing that there are invisible, conscious entities that move through the same spaces that we do in our daily lives. It's too much—too different from what we've been taught to believe. And so we file anything we hear about in that arena as a "ghost story." They are great for telling around the campfire, but anyone over thirteen who actually believes them has to be a little silly.

Perhaps it would help the reader to consider these beings "psychological allegories" as suggested in the narrative. This was my own favorite way to deal with them for many years. It took awhile to get it through my hard head that there are things that act like spirits—no matter what we choose to call them.

Ancestor spirits are perhaps the easiest to accept and to connect with. These spirits are different from ghosts. Rather than haunting the world of the living, they generally stay in the underworld, with the rest of the ancestor spirits. However, they remain connected to the world of their descendants and continue to have an impact on us. They can "hear" you when you call to them and they tend to offer their blessings in response to gifts and to being honored in other ways. To begin building a relationship with your ancestors, you can create an altar in your home dedicated to them. Place old photos or some symbolic representative of these ancestors on the altar along with whatever you want to offer them. It could be a bowl of water, a candle, flowers—just make it something that you think they would enjoy and not be offended by. For instance, if you know that your great grandmother was a teetotaler, don't offer her whisky.

Nature spirits come in a great variety. Historically they have been known as everything from pixies and faeries to ruchot and kontemoble. They tend to be connected with a particular natural setting, the boundaries of which may be defined by the land spirit, which is a different spirit all together. For instance, a river or spring might be considered a spirit as well. Most traditional cultures have means of maintaining peaceful relations with the nature spirits of their immediate surroundings. We can use a similar means of developing a peaceful and productive relationship with the nature spirits where we live. This can be as simple as setting out a bowl of milk on the back porch each evening, speaking out loud to the spirits and letting them know that this is offered as a gift for them. You might even go so far as to have a spirit house set up for them to live in. Just make sure that the shadow of your own house doesn't fall on the spirit house. This tends to make the spirits cross and they won't live there.

Both ancestor spirits and nature spirits respond well to your paying attention to them. Most of them are used to being ignored by humans in the West, but that doesn't mean that they like it. A simple gift of tobacco, water, incense or food can be a good start to building positive relationships with the spirits in your neighborhood.

Making an offering is a very easy. You call out loud to whatever spirit or spirits you wish to offer the gift to, and then you place that gift on the ground for them. You may also ask for a blessing, or simply offer it in gratitude.

In my own experience, the spirits like the attention and are generally willing to offer their blessings in return for feeling that you see and respect them. These blessings can be a powerful force. It means that the spirits will the energies around you to support your well being. They can just as easily will them to trip you up if you irritate them.

By connecting with the spirits around us, and the spirits of our ancestors, we not only create a better environment for us to live in, we also renew deeper connections within our own souls. When we pay attention to the spirits we begin to open our selves up to experience a larger, fuller and more beautiful world. That could be the greatest blessing in itself.

Chapter 15
Soli Dives in

We have stopped to take a break in Liskeard. Soli is just emerging from the phone box, snapping her wallet closed. "So much for keeping in touch with the office. I let them know that from now on, I'm really on holiday. It was either that or rent a new mobile phone."

Grinning to myself, I follow her across the car park toward a tourist center she has set her sights on.

We walk in, and Soli immediately applies herself to the wire racks of tour books, while I stretch out my lower back on the cold cement floor in the corner of the room.

Walking toward me, her nose in a guide book to Cornish spiritual sites, Soli asks, "What do you suppose 'Cornwall' means?"

"You mean beside the obvious—Wall of Corn?" I shrug. "Probably something to do with the old Celtic god Cernunos." Soli stares at me as if to determine my sincerity. "Why don't we ask someone here?" I continue.

Soli turns around and walks over to the service counter where I can see her speaking to the middle-aged woman in blue wool blazer. I can't hear what they are saying over the hum of the heating vent at my feet, but it's clear from the look on Soli's face as she returns that she did not get the answer she hoped for.

"Well?" I prompt.

"Wall of corn." Soli answers in a deadpan tone and goes back to her search for the perfect tour book.

I begin scanning a nearby rack myself, and find a slim chapbook, The Ancient Sites in West Penwyth, that looks interesting. As I open to the contents, I find 'fogous'. Curious about this strange word, I turn to page 31, where I read "Of all the different kinds of sites in Cornwall, perhaps fogous are the most special. They are (usually) curved underground passageways with a narrow side passage known as a creep sloping toward the surface...Entering them is like going into the womb of mother earth..."

Excited, I leaf ahead and sure enough there is the Boleigh Fogou. "The site lies in the grounds of the Rosemerryn House, so permission to visit must be obtained..." I go on to read that the fogou is variously thought to be an initiation chamber or a burial chamber. Unique to fogous (of which there seem to be a number in the neighborhood) Boleigh also has the upper part of a figure carved into the left hand entrance stone carrying a spear in one hand and a serpent in the other. I wonder if this is a depiction of the Celtic sun god Lugh.

A chill goes up my spine at this thought and I smile to myself in satisfaction. It seems like we are on the trail of something juicy. Closing the book, I place it back on the rack. I know now that I will find this place, and I have some small sense of what I will encounter there. But the rest of it will need to come from the place itself, not from a guide book.

"How is your foot holding up?" Soli asks. From the well–filled plastic sack fitting snugly under her arm, I see that she has made her purchases and is ready to move on.

"Well enough," I respond, climbing to my feet. "Besides, this floor is too hard to be comfortable for long."

Soli smiles and holds the door for me. We step out into a refreshingly dry afternoon. It has stayed sunny since we crossed the river which Soli has since informed me is the border between England and Cornwall.

"Okay!" Soli stands still on the sidewalk now, her back to the door we've just exited. "I want to try it."

"Try what?"

"I want to try 'feeling' for something."

"...Okay. What do you want to try feeling for?" I ask.

"I want to try to see if these 'feelings' and synchronicity are connected somehow. If I follow a 'feeling,' will it lead me to someplace that is connected to our journey?"

"Lead on," I reply. "Let your feelings be our guide."

Soli grins ferociously and sets off walking. I keep up with her as best I can, but soon she is pulling ahead. She pauses at each corner, then seems to get her bearings and sets off again. She is over a block ahead of me when I see her turn into a shop. When I come in the door, she is talking to a wiry older Cornishman who sits on a tall stool behind the wooden counter. She turns to me excitedly.

"He knows!" she says breathlessly. "The name Cornwall is an anglicized version of an older Celtic word that means 'eye of Kernunos'!"

"Now really—that's just a theory of my own..." the older gentleman tries to interject, but Soli isn't listening.

"It works! It works! I want to do more!" With this she grabs my hand and starts waltzing me around the small shop, filled with old sheet music displayed in glass cases. After a moment she realizes that I'm limping again and stops, but she is still excited and I can't help but enjoy her enthusiasm.

As we leave the shop, Soli stops and turns to me. "We're not looking for Ys anymore, are we?"

Her words strike a chord in me. I know that she is right. Our journey is leading us somewhere else now. It feels as if everything that came before was just to bring us here. "I guess not," I answer. "Are you alright with that?"

She nods thoughtfully. "It feels sad, but strangely. . . right." We walk on as this soaks in.

"So what is it that is happening when I do . . . what just happened?" Soli asks as we meander back slowly through the narrow streets.

"Everything is connected. You're tuning into the part of yourself that already knows that, and it's feeding you information. That's the underlying meaning of what we call synchronicity—the idea that every particle in the universe is, was, or will be in contact at with every other particle at some point within infinity—and so are connected now…remember your Carl Jung explanation…" We pause to wait for a break in the traffic before crossing the next street. "There are powerful places and powerful events in our lives that call to us, no matter where we are. We can learn to listen for and respond to that call. That's what is happening when you follow your feelings and they lead to synchronicity."

Crossing the road, Soli stops and looks around confused. "Do you think you can use your newly developed 'sixth sense' to find our car?" I ask mischievously.

Deepening

Carl Jung has his own theory of how synchronicity works: Within infinity, all particles of matter have been, are, or will be connected with one another, and this connection remains in a way that transcends time and space. When we perceive a synchronistic event, we are really just noticing the connections that are there all along.

Synchronicity is not what connects us. It is a theory that explains how we are connected. So when we talk about synchronicity, it naturally leads to a discussion of the interconnectedness of the universe.

To explore this quality of interconnection, I would like to remind you of the teaching of Grandfather's: There is only one center. It just happens to be everywhere. Since everything has a center, and all those centers are one center, everything is intimately connected to everything else in every moment—through that one center.

When Soli picks up the novel about the fabled city of Ys, she opens a doorway to these connections. At each step along our path she is extending her awareness to the connections that are already there. It's as if we have already made this journey and she is re–tracing our steps. The pattern is already there. The question becomes, are you willing to see it and to accept what it offers you?

This connection is of great use to the shaman. It allows us to recognize the patterns which weave the universe together, supporting life and bringing wave after wave of transformation—evolution—waves of forgetting and remembering. On our journey, we use this awareness to show us the next step along the path. Our willingness to take the path that is indicated opens us up to the adventure that is already there–awaiting our arrival.

Synchronicity can give us answers that go beyond the rational world of cause and effect. It reveals to us a world in which all things are connected.

Consider: There is only one center, and it is everywhere. It is in your own heart, but also at the heart of everything else. Every star, every stone, every tree and every person emerges from this very same center.

Synchronicity is not something we make happen. It is already there, all around us. It is the sensation we get when something feels "right." It is the shiver of energy that runs up our spine when we feel the pieces of a puzzle come together. Our openness to what is there—to synchronicity—gives us the ability to sense the existing connections between all the bits of the universe and to be guided by this awareness into the path of our own awakening.

To make use of it, all you have to do is pay attention. When you hold your awareness of the one center within you and then open your eyes and see that one center in everything around you – what do you notice? Your heartbeat? Your breath? The whole universe is breathing with you. Feel that connection. Know that you are not alone.

Go for a walk. What do you notice? The grass, a stone, a bottle, a lost toy. Every bit of the universe is reflected in every other bit.

Keep your heart open as you pay attention to what your eye is drawn to. You hear a bird squawk in the tree above you. You look up and the clouds are rolling past you. What does your heart tell you? Can you hear it? Are you willing to listen?

Keep your body open as you listen. Pay attention with all your senses. Feel the earth beneath you. Pick up that stone. Hold it in your hand. Listen to it. Can you feel it breathing with you? Can you feel the rhythms of its journey?

Ask the stone to listen to your journey as well. Does this seem absurd? Then laugh! (And the stone laughs with you.)

Chapter 16
A Hidden Treasure

Driving out of Liskeard, the sun still bright overhead, we plunge into a tunnel of huge old trees lining both sides of the narrow road. Their powerful limbs join overhead in a thick roof of leaves. The foliage is a blood green that feels magickal and deep.

Soli is still driving, though I have promised to take my turn tomorrow. So far, it seems pretty simple. Just remember to keep to the left.

We are both quiet now, but I think I can feel Soli appreciating the beauty and intensity of the land as well. It is so rich, so drenched with life force, that it is actually feeding us energy as we pass through it. Already I feel a little light headed from breathing in the abundance of Qi.

If anything, the almost kinesthetic sense that we are 'going the right way' is increasing, along with the excitement of what we might find. We are no longer on a search for Dahut's Ys. That search has led us to a deeper place of exploration. The story we are living seems to be changing as we go, revealing more faces and more secrets at every turn. As I feel this idea settling in my belly, we pass a sign for 'Carn Glaze Caverns.' A black and white bird leaps into the air from the sign and swoops across the road behind us.

"Slow down a bit," I tell Soli. "I want to see if we can find those caverns." I have a feeling that we need to take our journey underground somehow and the black and white bird catches my attention as well.

Soli slows just in time. As we round the next bend there is a small road off to the right, with a sign set in rusting iron. We take the turnoff and find ourselves on a very narrow road running alongside a winding creek. Before long, we come to a steep drive off to the right with an iron gate and a sign saying "Caverns closed." We slow down to read the sign, but the road is too tight to turn here, so we drive on. Coming to another turn off to the left, Soli slowly turns us in over an old stone bridge and into an even tinier lane. It feels as if we are being drawn into a net.

We drive on slowly, still looking for a place wide enough to turn around. An old stone farm house appears next to the road on the left, and another to the right. Then we come to a slight widening in the road, where an old collie lies sleeping in the sun. There is a wide double gate right before the napping dog. The sign on the wall reads "Lantern Mill B&B". Soli turns the car in through the gate, expecting to back out and turn around.

As we pass through the gate, it's as if we are entering another world. From the ancient farm road outside, we emerge into a scene out of a Faerie tale. There is a stream fed mill pond, with grassy banks and an old weeping willow shading most of it. A mixed family of swans and ducks are afloat on the pond and its calm, purplish surface reflects a swath of butter colored narcissus on the far side. At the foot of the cobbled drive, over–looking the pond, is a single slender iron lamp post, standing as if at sentry duty.

Soli and I have both stepped out of the car and are taking in this scene when we are startled by the sound of a door closing. A stout young woman is approaching us from the house, wiping flour from her hands on the apron she wears.

"Would you be wanting a room?" she asks with a smile.

Soli and I barely need to exchange a glance before agreeing to this, and we find ourselves shortly climbing a small spiral stair to our suite. Carefully negotiating our luggage through the narrow doorway, I find Soli already brewing a cup of tea from the bedside electric kettle.

"We are going to go back out aren't we?" she asks. "I don't want to miss the chance to stretch my legs."

"There's supposed to be some great stone sites on the Bodmin Moor," I reply. "Which can't be far from here. But I think I'll join you in a tea first." The child inside me is very excited about our finding this wonderful place, apparently by accident, and is eager to explore, but other parts of me just want to soak it up for a bit.

As we sit waiting for our tea to steep and looking out the window at our newly discovered view, Soli asks, "So what's the next step in learning how to journey like you do?" She turns to look at me. "I've been practicing the stillness exercise—at least a few times. But how do you get out of your body—or do you go out of your body?"

Setting my cup aside, I say, "Let's give it a try. Why don't you grab that pillow off the bed and get into a comfortable position on the floor. You want to be sitting up, with your back erect."

Soli folds the bed pillow under her on the floor and straightens her spine. Closing her eyes, she nods that she is now ready for me to begin the exercise.

"Begin by going into Stillness in your heart center. . . now more deeply. . . deeper still, looking for the doorway there. . . . As you reach the doorway, just rest there a bit. Let go of any thoughts. Now reach out and open the door." I can sense a shift as she does this, and I wait for it to subside.

"When you feel ready, go ahead and move through the door. Feel the sensation of moving from one side of the door to the other. Can you feel that?" After a moment, Soli nods slightly. I have her move in and out a few more times to familiarize her with the process.

"The side of the door you entered from is your outer body. The side of the door that you passed through into is your inner body. Just as your outer body is your access to the outer world, your inner body is your access to the inner world. Do you understand?" She shrugs then nods.

"This doorway lies at the center of everything. You don't need to understand that now, but remember it for later. You might also notice that there is a lot of energy coming out of the doorway on either side. This is undifferentiated Qi that comes from between these two worlds. Now—keeping yourself focused on the inner side of the door—take some of that Qi and shape it into a large, full length mirror right in front of you. Make it close enough to touch." I can feel her reaching out with her energy, hesitantly at first, to shape a mirror.

"Feel your reflection in the mirror. Don't worry if you don't see anything there. Just be aware that there is—something—in the mirror. Let that something have form, substance, presence." I wait until I can feel that presence take form in her mirror. "That's it. Stay in your heart center for now, but reach out with a strand of the Qi— the radiance emerging from that center—and touch the surface of the mirror. Set any doubt aside and just let it happen. Let yourself take in the information, the sensation of that surface. Now penetrate the mirror with your beam of light. Move through the surface and onward until you touch this presence on the other side. Plug this tendril of light into the heart center of this reflection, this other "you" that is on the far side of the mirror.

"Pay attention to where you are in your physical body...and now, just like you would move your attention from your head down into your heart, go ahead and move your attention from your own heart center, down that line of light...through the surface of the mirror." My own body jumps suddenly as I feel her penetrate the mirror and pass through into her Shamanic Body. ". . . and on through the heart center of your Shamanic Body. Find that same doorway here. . . And open it. . . And pass through. Now let yourself emerge through that center and out into this other form. Allow yourself to get used to it gradually—gently. This is your Shamanic Body. Just as your physical body is who you are in the physical realm—this is who you are here in the shamanic reality of the three worlds."

Quickly, I move through into my own center and extend into my Shamanic Body. Opening my senses here in the shamanic lodge, I 'see' Soli near me, sitting on the earthen floor of the lodge. I move over to her and begin to speak to her both in the lodge and in the physical body. "You're doing really well. Just let yourself feel what it's like to be in this body now. Why don't you try to rub your hands together?" I see her try to do this, but the palms of her hands are not yet solid enough, so they keep sliding through one another. I reach out and hold them, solidify them a bit and she can begin to feel the texture of her skin. This draws her more deeply into the experience and I see her begin to smile in her Shamanic Body.

Gradually I lead Soli through some more exercises to accustom her to this new body. I ask her to explore the textures of her skin on her face and arms; to run her fingers through her hair—which she discovers is much longer in her Shamanic Body. Finally I lead her back out through the mirror and into her physical body, and I follow her out into my own physical form.

As I open my eyes, Soli is pouting. "What's wrong?" I ask.

"My tea got cold." She replies, then smiles brightly.

Deepening

A curious thing happened when Grandfather taught me how to move into my shamanic body. First of all, I discovered that I have a different body that I can move into whenever I want to and that I can use this body to go on shamanic journeys. This immediately transformed my practice of journeying and I realized that all I had been doing up until then was creative visualization. While that is also a powerful and effective tool, it is different from what I was able to do once I learned how to move out of the physical body and into shamanic body.

This was all great, but the really curious thing was that every time I moved into my shamanic body, it was always in the same place: A large domed chamber, with a huge tree growing up from the floor and out through ceiling. To this day, I don't really know why it works this way. I suppose it's one of the Mysteries. Grandfather talks about this space as the Lodge, so I've taken to calling it Shamanic Lodge.

You may recall the earlier discussion of how shamans from all over the world share similar maps that include three worlds with something connecting them. One of the ways of connecting the three worlds is the World Tree. The tree growing up through the Lodge is just that: The World Tree. It wasn't long after finding my way there that Grandfather introduced me to the Tree and then reached into it and drew out what looked and felt like liquid light. He pulled at this substance like taffy, creating strands that he braided into a cord. Then he reached into me—which was an interesting sensation—and tied one end of the cord around my spine so that it came out through my navel and extended on into the Tree.

This was all rather strange, and I didn't know what to make of it. Grandfather had me feel the cord and after some time, I was able to feel a pulse. It was as if there was blood running through the cord. I thought of the umbilical cord that connects mother to child in her womb. Grandfather smiled and nodded, apparently reading my mind.

Experience taught me that this cord not only provides me with a permanent connection to the World Tree, it also can feed me energy from the Tree and keep me from getting lost on my journeys into the three worlds. That's a pretty special cord. On top of all that, it can completely disappear when I'm not paying attention to it, but it pops back in as soon as I need it. And when I find myself out somewhere very strange and I'm not sure how to find my way back to the Lodge, I can grab ahold of the cord, give it a sharp jerk and it draws me back into Lodge. Very handy.

I've been saving the best for last. The Tree itself is amazing. Grandfather taught me how to open the Tree and move into it so that I can travel down into the Under World or up into the Upper World. It offers a safe and simple route to all three worlds. The Middle World is just outside the Lodge and I reach it by opening doors through the walls of the Lodge.

Fortunately, Grandfather's teachings seem to apply to others as well. When I show my students how to access their shamanic bodies, they also appear in Lodge. With practice, all of them are able to interact with the Tree and they are usually able to see me and others in their shamanic bodies there too.

I have found versions of this teaching in traditional shamanic practices. Like the maps of the three worlds, there are some differences, but the basics are the same.

While we don't talk much about shamanic journeying in this narrative, it is an important tool for the modern shaman. And like everything else, all the shaman's tools are interconnected. Learning about journeying in shamanic body helps you to understand other parts of the map as well.

Chapter 17
Into the Labyrinth

As we walk past the kitchen door on our way to the car, our hostess, Diane, turns from her cutting board. "Do you know when you'll be wanting your breakfast?"

"At about eight, I think," I reply. "Would you happen to know of any stone circles around this area?"

"Of course." She sets down her mixing bowl and comes to join us in the doorway. "The best is 'the Hurlers' up on the moor. You could walk to it if you've a mind, but it's probably best you drive. Just go back to the motorway; take a left and then another left to St. Neots, then follow the signs." This all sounds easy enough. As we turn back to the car, we see another one of the black and white birds sitting on the lamp post. After a moment it springs off the pole and swoops away over the pond.

"What kind of bird is that?" I ask, pointing after the disappearing shape.

"Oh that's a magpie. There quite common here." She smiles and returns to her kitchen.

Soli drives as we retrace our way, past the sleeping collie, back across the narrow bridge and onto the winding one–lane road. The sun is still coming through the multi–green of the trees, dappling the road in front of us with its light.

"Details," I say.

"Hmmm?" asks Soli.

"Details. You have to pay attention to the details." I repeat. "Look where we're headed—what do you see?"

"...the road. Trees. Stone wall. Man with a wheel barrow..."

"What color is it?"

"Green–ish yellow."

"Good! And?"

"Dead. . . . something by road. Dead tree. Sign."

"Okay," I say. "How much of that do you remember now?"

"The man with the puke green wheel barrow. . . The stone wall...."

"That's how easy it is to not see. All that stuff was there. We drove right past it, but if you hadn't made a real effort to pay attention to the details, it would have all been a blank."

"Am I missing something here?" Soli asks.

"No, no—I was just thinking about a complaint I often hear in my workshops, that it is so hard to see anything in the shamanic body. But it's hard to see anything in the physical body too—if you're not paying attention."

We follow the signs through the narrow lanes, with hedgerows towering above us on either side, to St. Neot's. From there we take what seems to be the obvious route and proceed to spend two and a half hours lost in a maze of farms, hedgerows and magpies.

Often it is the magpies that lead us on to what seems like the right path, until we come to another village and see that we are somewhere we didn't intend to be. We seem to be looping back and forth through the same places, and yet missing the door we are looking for. Are we not "supposed" to find the Hurlers? I begin to think of Faerie and the myths of hidden doorways into the mysterious lands under the mountain.

Rather than getting frustrated, I take this as a sign that we need some extra help. I ask Soli to pull off the narrow road near a crossing and after digging in my daypack, I hop out into the crossroads. I hold a pinch of tobacco into the air and say, "Hello, Spirits. Spirits of the crossroads—spirits of this place. I offer you this tobacco. Please accept this gift and bless us, help us to find our way." Sprinkling the tobacco over the crossroads, I feel a subtle sense that the offering is received.

As I am walking back to the car, I notice an elderly gentleman in a tweed jacket and cap walking toward us along the hedgerow. I say "hello" and find that he just happens to have a surveyor's map of the area tucked in his pocket. One look at the highly detailed map explains why we've had such a devil of a time finding the place. The roads here are so twisted back on one another that the map looks like a plate full of spaghetti. It doesn't help that the hedgerows are so high on either side of the narrow and twisty road that you can't see what's coming around the bend until it's in your face. With a quick murmur of thanks to the spirits, I climb back into the car and we are off again, but with much clearer direction.

Arriving at the pull off for the Hurlers, we see a tour bus and a few other cars. I'm amazed that the buses have managed to reach this point and I assume that there is some other more accessible route that we've missed. I stop for a moment to look at the sign for the Hurlers, which includes an artist rendering showing, not one but three circles, placed one above the other. "Just like a map of the three worlds," I think.

The grass is incredibly green, soft and lumpy. There are divots the size of cantaloupes and watermelons and beachballs. There are round ridges where the grass has worn off, revealing hard bare dirt like the heads of bald old men.

My right foot still aches and it doesn't like the idea of walking across all this lovely lumpy grass. The pain has made its way up into the muscles between the bones in my arch and seems to want to set up housekeeping there. Strangely, it doesn't respond to the sort of energetic manipulation I would expect it to. I've tried getting it to open and flow, but it just ignores me. And then sometimes it just disappears for awhile—only to show up again later, when I'm beginning to think it's gone for good.

As we walk slowly toward the circles, I notice that the sky is turning a deep and meaningful grey, and moving closer and closer to the ground.

We approach the stones, strange grey lumps of dough in a field of green, just as the tourists are rounding themselves up into groups and heading back to their bus.

We pause outside the stones, waiting for the last of the other visitors to leave. While we wait, I notice a dark grey stone peeking through the grass, but masked with lichen. I sit down beside it on the damp grass and let my senses reach into the stone. I can feel it resting deep into the earth. It is a large one; perhaps as much as eight feet tall, with only this cap showing above the grass. Feeling the power it has gathered from being so long in the earth, I decide to see if it might have a little extra to share. I take off my sandal and rest my aching foot against the lichen encrusted stone. It is cool and rough to the touch, and I silently ask it to help heal my foot, but I don't seem to be getting much in the way of an answer. There is only the slightest buzz of energy through the deeper part of the rock, and that seems more of a distant radio station than a present healer. I sigh and pull my sandal back on and stand up to join Soli, who is looking at me suspiciously.

We stand and watch a pair of sheep, one of which is rubbing itself against the center stone of the middle ring. A brown pony is nosing in the grass as a couple with their basset hound approach along the path leading up to the ridge beyond us. The pony apparently hears the couple and sidesteps around in a circle before abandoning his patch of grass and ambling off. The sky is a curious mixture of small, disorderly clouds and a uniform blueish grey haze that seems full of wet, but not quite ready to rain.

The stones are set in three rings along a wide, sloping ridge. The middle ring is the largest and has a solid center stone. The lower ring is smaller and only a few stones are still standing. The rest seem to have sunk back into the earth. The upper ring—also smaller—is directly up the slope and still has all its stones. Soli and I stand here at the edge until the couple and their hound disappear over the moor.

"I've got an idea for an impromptu ritual of sorts. Why don't you enter through the upper circle of stones and I'll go in through the lower circle. Both of us make a complete circuit of those stones and then come to the middle circle, where we circle those stones and then meet at the center stone?" Soli shrugs and moves off in the direction indicated.

I head down to the lower circle and there is a sensation like passing through the surface of a mirror as I slip across the outer edge. I feel myself in the lower world, and I realize in my bones that this is a map of the three worlds. I was thinking it might be, but now there's no question. The truth of it is right here. I can smell it in the earth and read it in the scraps of sheep's wool scrubbed off onto the rough stones. I touch what I can of the ones that are still peeking above the ground, and feel the rest of them beneath me, as I walk across them.

As I touch each stone, I feel them hook up into a wheel of energy. When I come back to the first stone, this wheel is completed and begins to spin; slowly at first, then faster. It's like watching a propeller that spins faster and faster until it seems to change directions. The same thing happens to the energy of the circle, and now I can feel it flowing in both directions at once. The energy is comfortable and stable. It feels like it is used to working like this—but out of practice.

I turn and see that Soli is moving into the middle circle now, so I head in as well. Since Soli is passing along the outside of the stones, walking clockwise and tracing her fingers across the surface of each stone as she passes, I walk counter clockwise and to the inside.

Once again, I can feel the energies hook up as we string the stones together. Passing Soli, I can feel her doing the same thing, whether she realizes it or not. As we complete our circuits, we both move to the center stone together. I can feel what Soli has brought with her from the upper circle. I can feel it mix and harmonize with what I bring in from the lower circle. And now I sit down beside the stone, because all this spinning has me more than a little dizzy. Soli sits solemnly across from me and we both rest our hands on the center stone. I rest my forehead lightly against its surface. A moment later, I hear Soli start to giggle. I look up and she is bushing.

"I'm sorry—it tickles!" She explains.

Laughing, I squeeze her hands and reply, "It does, doesn't it."

"What did we just do?" she asks smiling again.

"The map of the shaman says there are three worlds that we live in. Most of us only recognize the middle world, but we all interact with the upper and lower worlds as well," I tell her.

"You mean—like these three rings here..." Soli begins.

"Yes. It's like a map. And the stones in the center of each ring represent the world tree that joins the three worlds together. But it's hard to put the ritual of joining the three worlds into a rational explanation." I pause to consider how to put it into words, but another couple appears over the ridge above us, with two dogs weaving toward us, noses to the ground. "I think we'd better close down this space and head back to the car."

"How do we close it down?"

"Go into your center." I wait until I can feel her focus enter her heart center. "Now open the doorway there...that's it." I can feel her already beginning to move through. "Just reach out around you. Feel how you have extended into the space around the stones. . . Bring that energy back in through this doorway at your center and release it into your body."

As I feel her begin to follow my suggestion, I go ahead and bring my own energy in as well, leaving the energies of the stones up and spinning. As Soli's eyes flicker open, I squeeze her hands again and release them. "Very good. You're a natural."

She smiles and helps me up. For all the energy work we've just done, my foot is aching more than ever. As I limp back toward the car, Soli asks, "Why was my energy just in the middle circle? I walked around the upper one as well."

"And when you touched the center stone of the middle circle, you brought that whole circle down there—just as I brought the lower one up. It is a joining of the three worlds—that allows for the . . . Magickal qualities of the upper and lower worlds to be more accessible in the middle one."

"Right." Soli fishes the car keys out of her jacket pocket. "I hope you don't expect me to be satisfied with that answer."

"Of course not," I grin. "But it will all become clearer eventually."

Soli hurumphs as she opens the doors. Somehow, we manage to drive back to St. Neot's in only fifteen minutes—as opposed to the over two hours it took to find our way here. There is only one pub in the village and we are hoping that it will still be open and it is— barely. We slip behind a narrow wooden table in the dining room and signal the waitress that we want menus.

"I didn't think we'd make it," Soli tells me confidentially, hoping that the waitress won't overhear and get any bright ideas like telling us that the kitchen is closed for the evening. We get our menus and with them, another surprise. The menu lists things like raspberry truffles, corn souffle, vegetarian lasagna and ratatoui— not at all what we expected from a small town Cornish pub.

When the food comes, it's excellent. It turns out that the pub has a professional chef, and after all the turmoil leading up to this moment—it feels like this is a reward of sorts. And a well deserved one at that.

As we dig into our vegetarian lasagna, enjoying the rich flavors and textures of the food, I notice a couple at a table along the wall. They are being physically demonstrative in a very un–English sort of way. Visibly affectionate, him holding her hand and her blushing and smiling and laughing.

Soli notices my attention and follows my gaze to the couple against the wall. She frowns as if irritated by the sight. After a few moments she comments, "I think they must be tourists—or on their honeymoon." From her tone, I've no doubt that she disapproves.

"Weren't you a tourist when we met?" I ask, nodding toward the couple.

"Was not!" Soli replies defiantly. "I am never a tourist. I was doing research in a foreign country." But I can see her smile now. "You're the tourist," she teases me.

"Why? Because I took you up on your invitation to visit?

"Why did you come? Soli asks.

"It was an opportunity—I don't mean that I've never had other opportunities. I mean that it was an open door that felt right." I stop to consider and chew another bite. "It felt unique and familiar at the same time. That caught my attention. Also, I wanted to explore what connection I felt with you, since it was obviously not a romantic one. I'm really not in the market for any of that at the moment."

Soli smirks and is silent for a long moment, taking another bite of lasagna and chewing it well then setting her fork aside. When she speaks, her eyes are still focused down at her plate and her voice is so low that I have to lean toward her to hear what she's saying.

"The reason I was able to take this time off from work—the reason I chose to—is that there is an uncomfortable situation for me there." She is quiet for another minute. She takes a sip from her glass, then "There is an older man who works there. He does things like changing the toner in the copiers." Soli is blushing now and her voice has become even softer.

"Yes...?" I encourage her.

"I find him. . . strangely . . . attractive. Like a dream almost." She turns to me now, searching my face for understanding. "It feels like I've known him before, and every time I see him, I feel...strange and scared and alive..."

"It almost sounds like you're in love," I say, being careful not to laugh. I suspect this is really hard for her.

"But I don't even know the man!" she hisses. "He's nothing like what I would want in a partner."

"How do you know?"

She glares at me. "...Know?"

I begin hesitantly, "well, you just said that you didn't—"

"He's just a common worker. He doesn't have a university degree, or he wouldn't be changing toner cartridges, so he can't be all that bright! And I'm not about to have anything to do with someone who can't respect me as their equal!" I wait for the steam to clear a bit before I respond.

"Sometimes the people we fall in love with have more to do with our own internal mysteries than they do with—"

Soli cuts me off with another glare. "I was hoping for something a little less banal from you. I know he probably reminds me of something in my unconscious or whatever. That's not really helpful. What I want to know is what do I do about it?"

Deepening

As mentioned in the previous deepening, the World Tree in Lodge connects the three worlds — Upper, Middle and Lower. These three worlds are the territory the shaman travels through in search of healing, lost power and realization. All three worlds have a lot in common. Each has ground and sky, with everything that entails. In fact, they can often appear identical. However the nature of each is significantly different.

The Middle world is essentially a reflection of what you see around you in your ordinary state of consciousness. You can travel to any place you have experienced in your life on this planet and still be in the Middle World. Along with the humans, animals and other obvious inhabitants, you can also find various nature spirits. These spirits are often more easy to interact with while in shamanic consciousness.

The Upper World is a more rarefied space. While it generally appears as the upper limbs of a gigantic tree or like the classical visions of heaven, complete with cloud banks and alabaster benches, exploration reveals that it too has ground, water and even good solid dirt to dig into. Never–the–less, when it comes to animals, it does seem to be home to mostly birds.

This Upper World also holds what we often refer to as ascended masters — those who have evolved to a level of consciousness where they are able to maintain awareness without taking on a physical body. These can be very helpful teachers, and are sought after by any who would learn about the mysteries of the Upper World especially.

Here also are the souls of those who are in between incarnations. These are the strands on which the pearls of the many lifetimes we live are strung.

The animals that appear in the Middle World are all connected with a Great animal spirit that resides in the Lower World. The many deer that you may encounter in the middle world are all connected with the single Deer spirit in the Lower World.

The Lower World is where our spirits go when our physical bodies die. This is where we join with our ancestors. It is also where we can journey in Shamanic Body to visit these ancestors – the spirits of those who came before us.

Chapter 18
Dreamtime

We arrive back at the Mill after dark and stand by the pond for a few minutes, soaking up the serenity before heading in for the night. Diane—our hostess—meets us as we come in and confirms our orders for breakfast, then we climb the stairs to our room.

Suddenly tired, I am tempted to flop onto the bed, but Soli is already digging through her shower kit and I know I should brush my teeth as well.

I brush and rinse and floss and am looking for a waste can to dispose of my used floss, when Soli speaks up.

"They must think we're either an old married couple or brother and sister."

"What do you mean?"

"I was thinking of that couple at the pub tonight. They were obviously lovers—probably just married, or having a wicked affair. We are—just as obviously—not lovers. I mean, people must be able to see that."

I smile. "You mean that you think they can sense our chemistry—or what?"

She grimaces. "Nothing so esoteric. It's how we act. We're comfortable with each other. We like each other, but you don't see us hugging and kissing and holding hands and blushing like that." She pauses then starts changing into her flannel nightshirt.

"Were you thinking of something in particular?" I ask.

Popping her head through the neck of the nightshirt, Soli replies, "I was just thinking about how a shaman views sex. Not like our last conversation about shamanic sex. I was just messing with you then."

"I suspected as much," I reply, grinning at her now.

She looks over at me now and seems to be almost blushing. "I couldn't imagine taking this trip with any of my other male friends—well, any of my other straight male friends—but it feels completely comfortable with you. Why is that?"

"Those are two very different questions," I reply. She sits on the foot of the bed and I join her. Taking her hand, I begin to work on a point between her thumb and forefinger that I can feel is clogged. "In the first place, we don't have that kind of chemistry. You said it yourself before. It would be – untrue. . . unauthentic for us to be sexual. It would be communicating something that is not there. A lie. We both have good enough boundaries that we can see that and act toward each other appropriately—agreed?"

Wincing a bit from my pressure on her hand, Soli responds, "Agreed!"

"As to how shamans view sex—" I pause and sort my thoughts. This is a big subject and not something we can cover tonight. "It's easily one of the most important aspects of the human experience. It requires respect and clarity and understanding. But it doesn't really fit into the guidelines our society has laid out for it."

Satisfied that the blocked energy is flowing now, I let go of her hand and Soli shakes it out. "Go on," she says.

"Sexual feelings form the basis for our very existence in this world."

She holds up one finger to stop me. "Okay. You mentioned something like that before and I have a problem with that. I think my life is pretty full and good and I haven't had sex in—quite a long time."

"No," I reply. "But your sexual feelings, your creative juices, if you will, continue to fuel your work."

"Well naturally—that's what I like to call 'work eros.'" Soli adds.

"Exactly. Sexual feelings don't necessarily have anything to do with being sexual with another person. But they still make us feel powerful and alive. And when they get blocked, we feel powerless and frustrated." I reach over and poke a finger into her butt cheek. She yelps.

"Hey! That hurts!"

"That's one of the spots that gets sore when you're repressing your sexual energy. If you keep it up long enough, you can give yourself sciatica."

"Well, what am I supposed to do about it?" she asks, rubbing her hip and glowering at me.

I laugh. "You don't have to have sex—you don't even need to masturbate—to release sexual energy. You just need to allow yourself to feel it—and then direct it into doing something. You already do that a lot with your work—or that point would be a lot more painful."

Soli replies sulkily, "Lucky me! I still don't see how that makes sex so important."

"Okay—since I don't feel like talking about this all night, would you do an exercise with me?"

"That depends," She replies suspiciously.

"It won't hurt and it's not sexual—not overtly anyway." I reassure her. "Come on and lie back on the bed."

She makes herself comfortable and I sit next to her. "Everybody has a basic human need for touch," I begin. "If babies are not held enough, they don't develop. If we don't get touch as adults, we forget how to respond to others. We shut down, turn off and become depressed. Now just let yourself relax—and feel that need your body has for touch...trust me. We all have it."

We are quiet for a few minutes. I can feel Soli's thoughts start to wander but then she brings them back into focus of her own accord. A moment later, "I think I can feel it now. Its not very strong, but there is a part of me that kind of wants touch...I think."

"Just let yourself focus on that part of you. Let go of everything else for now. Let that part grow stronger and clearer. Listen to it and let it know that you are listening."

"...okay..."

I wait until I can feel her energy shifting deeper before I continue. "Begin to give that part of you the power to reach out into the world around you. Give it a little control over your body. Let it have your right arm and hand. Let it reach out with that arm and hand and take hold of my hand here...that's it." Slowly, Soli's right hand reaches out and finds my hand, grasping it lightly. "Now feel that hunger for touch and let it direct that touch back to your body to complete the circuit—to feel the fulfillment of that need."

Soli does not respond right away. I am almost ready to begin repeating myself, when her hand begins to slowly tug mine in toward her body, bringing it to her abdomen and resting it there. I wait for the energy to begin flowing in response, but it doesn't. "Let your body feel that response." I prompt. "Let yourself feel the touch that you have directed back to you. This is your power in the world. Your ability to meet your need for touch." Now I can feel things begin to stir. "Let that energy you're feeling now continue to direct that touch..." After another minute, she begins to move my hand in a slow circle around her navel. I can feel her moving deeper into herself and dropping out of her conscious mind. Since I don't want to stir things up too much tonight, I decide to finish up now.

"Let yourself direct that touch in a way that brings you into balance with it—so that you can release the touch—letting go of it in a way that leaves you energized and comfortable..." She moves my hand slowly up to her heart chakra, then lifts it off and lets it go.

"Don't drift off to sleep just yet. Come on back up," I tell her. "You'll want to integrate some first."

Soli's eyes flutter open and, after another moment she looks over to me. "How do you feel?" I ask.

"Kind of warm and. . . dopey," she replies.

"Okay—anything else?"

She closes her eyes again to consider this, and I'm afraid she will fall asleep, but she opens them again and says, "It doesn't make any sense, but I feel more. . . real."

I smile, glad to hear that it's getting through to her. "Okay. It does make sense— but it might be awhile before you look at 'sense' that way. Why don't you sleep on it now?"

"Good idea," she murmurs and closes her eyes again.

I lean back and pull the down bed cover up over my arms, warming my body from inside out with my breath. I can feel something nudging me—but I can't feel what it is —and I'm too exhausted right now to try and sort it out.

As I drop into sleep, I move through my inner doorway, through my Shamanic Body and into my Dream Body. I lose focus for awhile, then find myself digging in a cavern. There are precious gems and other treasures here. I know that from past visits. And at some level, I know that I am dreaming and that this is a place that I visit when I am looking for parts of myself that have been buried.

Beautiful green and purple, faceted stones as big as my fist pop to the surface as I dig deeper, but these don't feel like what I'm looking for. Feeling frustrated, I leave the stones and walk deeper into the cavern, which gradually narrows into a tunnel that slopes downward into the earth. For some reason, I am feeling anger— hot rage tinged with fear pulsing through me—and just as suddenly, it is gone. The tunnel opens into a colonnade, which is part of an old school. I keep trying to focus on why I'm here, but I don't remember this place. I know that I was supposed to learn something here, but all I can remember is that I have not yet learned it and that "I" am not the "I" that was here before.

I wander into a large open space that feels like a gymnasium, with tiled floors. In the middle of the space, a young tree has pushed up through the tiles, shoving them aside and growing straight and true. Even as I watch it seems to continue to grow taller and taller.

There is a sense of someone behind me and I turn to find Grandfather watching me from the doorway. I'm relieved to see him. "I was looking for you!" I exclaim.

"Were you?" he asks and comes toward me.

"Maybe not," I reply, suddenly confused.

Grandfather laughs, a short soft bark, then walks toward me. He is dressed in overalls, like a mechanic, and he looks different. He actually looks like an old man, instead of like a spirit dressed up to look like an old man. I can see the furrows in his cheeks and smell the acrid sweat of his body.

He squats down beside me and lifts my foot, as if he was checking the hoof of a lame horse. "Why have you wounded yourself, eh?" he asks. "Maybe just to bring you here, hmmm?" He sets my foot down. "That's right," I think. "I hurt my foot on the beach, and it must be still hurting in my sleep."

I am feeling the anger again, and this time more of the fear as well. My heart is cold in my chest and I recognize this fear. Something very old. Something I have avoided for a very, very long time.

I realize that I am walking down the tunnel again. The anger is past for the moment, but the floor of the tunnel is wet and I am still limping. The wet floor is becoming slippery, so I reach out to the walls of the tunnel which narrow to accommodate me. As I touch the walls, they seem to move beneath my fingers. The left wall slowly writhes as if it is filled with serpents and the right wall pulses as if it is one great heart, pounding blood through a huge body.

The water grows steadily deeper until it is up to my ankles, but it is very cold and it seems to be taking the pain out of my foot, so I don't mind. There is a whisper of voices around me, but I see no one. They seem to speak, but I cannot understand their words. They call me deeper....

Deepening

Many people in the West have at least heard of the aboriginal concept of the Dreamtime. This is not to be confused with the dreamscape that you visit in your Dream Body, or the internal space where you stir up your own inner dreamings.

Dreamtime is another Mystery all its own.

Dreamtime is the underlying substance that we all emerge from. It is the place before time began. It is the place that is not a place—the time that is not a time. It exists everywhere and in everything, but can be found nowhere at all.

Only by coming to live in a world of Mystery, by coming to appreciate the things that are larger than our capacity to understand in a rational manner, can you really begin to encounter the Dreamtime. Then it will appear beside you; suddenly you realize that it has always been there. You reach to grasp it; it is gone and has never been.

Mysteries don't come to you when you call. They respond to surrender—to letting go of all understanding, knowledge and the hunger for knowing. They often appear when you are exhausted from seeking them—when you have given up the search.

It is the hunger that hides them. It is the shadow that reveals them.

Dreamtime is perhaps the greatest Mystery, since it is the source of the Mysteries—and everything else. Our hunger to be born, to live and thrive, calls us from the Dreamtime—just as our parents hunger for each other, calls us into this world.

Like all Mysteries, Dreamtime cannot be understood intellectually. But you can hold in your mouth and savor it. It will reveal itself to you as you open yourself to it. You may find yourself returning to it before you know.

What Dreamtime has in common with the more ordinary dreaming that we do while asleep is the sense that we have encountered a different but equally valid experience of reality.

Chapter 19
Staying in Practice

I wake up the next morning to silence, which concerns me. So far, each morning, I've been roused from sleep by Soli's snoring in the bed beside me. Imagining she might already be outside, and that I've somehow overslept, I throw on my favorite mindless attire— my cargo pants and dojo t-shirt—and make my way to the dining room. I'm immediately greeted by our landlady, Diana, who graciously hands me coffee as soon as I see her. "How did you know?" I smile, and she blushes and turns away. "By the way…" I ask, "have you seen my friend this morning?" She raises her eyebrows and shakes her head.

Although the morning is grey and cold, I decide to have my coffee on the back porch at the edge of the mill pond. It looks like the sky is about to burst with rain but I take my chances. I hope, that I'll see Soli there; I'm a little worried about her.

Out on the porch, there's an old German couple sitting quietly with their aging dachshund between them. While I enjoy the sense of peace and affection that rests between them, and even have a pang of unresolved grief as I remember my own grandparents, who have long passed, I am ultimately distracted by Soli's whereabouts. I have never, so far on this trip, woken up and not found her there. In fact, we even have our own morning routine now.

First, we meditate, which usually involves nothing more ceremonious than me rolling up a hotel towel under me to act as a meditation pillow and Soli folding her pillow in half and sitting on that. Actually I'm surprised that Soli was willing to try meditating, but she had done some before, as 'research' of course.

We sit facing the wall of our room. The view doesn't really matter since with this version of meditation your eyes are closed and your whole focus is internal. We do some yoga breathing that I've shared with Soli to get ourselves focused and then we move into Stillness. We spend at least ten minutes sitting like this. It wasn't until yesterday morning that Soli finally asked me why it's so important that we do this every morning. I suspect she just wanted her tea earlier.

I told her that I do it because I feel lousy if I don't do it.

"But why would you feel lousy?" she asked.

I thought about it for a moment, letting my mind shift into a more verbal gear. "I know I've said before that there's only one center—and it's everywhere, but if I don't pay attention and hook into that center on a regular basis, it's very easy to lose myself in the outside world." Soli doesn't seem completely convinced of my argument and I feel like I'm not really being clear about what it means to me either—so I dig deeper.

"There are all sorts of reasons why it's important to keep an awareness of the larger world—the world that exists through that center—but what it really comes down to is the old 'use it or lose it' thing. If I don't keep up a regular practice of Stillness and everything else I do, I lose my ability to function in that larger world. And I'm not much use to anyone as a shaman if I can't get out my own door."

"So it's not to achieve enlightenment?" she asked. She rushed over to turn the tea kettle on; it was clear that tea took precedence over any discussions of enlightenment.

Smiling, I replied. "Oh, I think achieving enlightenment is just something that happens when you stay centered long enough—whether you think you're looking for it or not."

"So—I guess what I'm really asking is why should I—or anyone—do this sort of thing? Is it just part of being a shaman?"

Her questions felt heavy, and I was tempted to ask her to put them off until after I'd had my coffee and we were on the road again. But like all good questions, it had already started gnawing at me, making me think more than I'd like to that early.

"People have some funny ideas about enlightenment—and about shamanism, for that matter. Most Westerners have this idea that there is some secret critical mass of meditative bliss they have to achieve, at which point they will miraculously split open and a neon lotus will pop out, with a blinking sign that says 'Congratulations! You have achieved nirvana!' Personally, I'm not even sure I would want nirvana. What I do want is to keep growing, keep exploring this larger world I talk so much about."

Not one to be put off, Soli asked yet again. "But just what is enlightenment then—and what does it have to do with shamanism?"

"Enlightenment is, very simply, being awake. Being awake in the fullest sense. What we think of as 'being awake'—when we're walking around in our daily lives—is really just a very deep dream state. Waking up means letting go of the idea that this is really all there is, that this—" I thumped the wall beside me. "—is reality. But it's not an intellectual realization—it's a realization that reaches through all of your senses and changes everything...while everything remains the same."

"So I guess you're not enlightened yet yourself?" Soli asked hesitantly.

"I sure don't feel like I am this morning," I said. After all, I already heard people milling around downstairs, and I really wanted that coffee; so much for being free of desire. Still, I went on to explain. "It's not an on or off sort of thing either. Like a lot of changes, it happens gradually and all at once—it can be sporadic, or tilt your awareness just enough that the things that used to drive you crazy don't bother you in the least anymore, but you still can't walk through walls—yet." I smiled. "As to what it has to do with shamanism—a shaman has to operate in that bigger world. That's where the spirits live, and where everything else we need to do our work is. But for a tribal shaman whose world already contains those spirits and such, it isn't a matter of awakening—just of staying awake."

While I am sometimes a little annoyed and exhausted by our conversations, this morning I miss her questions, as I sit on the porch, watching the old couple laughing at something no one around them would probably understand. Perhaps Soli was right; we are like an old married couple, the kind whose youthful attraction has transformed into a bloodless but deep affection. I'm feeling a bit overwhelmed by the depth of that affection when, true to the law of attraction, a figure resembling Soli slowly emerges from a grove of fir trees, not more than 30 feet away from me. At first, I begin to imagine that something tragic happened to her—

perhaps she went for a hike and fell; from this distance, her gait is like that of a wounded deer and I've never seen her walk so slowly. I immediately stand up and begin to walk toward her as quickly as I can while carrying a cup of hot coffee.

By the time I reach her, coffee–stained and a bit red–faced, she registers vague recognition of me. "Oh, hi," she says.

Her eyes are red and swollen and streaks of mud cover her face like war paint.

"Did you fall? Are you alright?" I ask, gently reaching for her arm.

"I'm fine," she says, unconvincingly.

"Do you want to tell me what might have happened in the woods?" By now, I'm getting the idea that she must be in a state of deep shock and denial, and that something traumatic must have happened on her walk.

Fortunately, my question only makes her laugh. "Kenn, nothing happened in the woods. I…I called into work."

"In the woods?" I begin. I'm beginning to think that Soli can find a phone anywhere.

"No! Not in the woods…Get out of the woods for a moment, will you? I've only been walking in the woods for about a half hour now. Before that, I called work, and finally explained to them, in greater detail you know, how I'd lost my mobile." She glares at me, as if I am the one responsible for her losing it, as if I personally hid the phone within a secret fold of the universe.

"And, they said, 'when we weren't able to get a hold of you, we figured it was reflective of your commitment to the station.' They sounded like a piece of textbook business correspondence. Suddenly, these people I work with—this guy I drink with on Fridays after work, that I've swapped gossipy e-mails with, that I even kissed once at the holiday party, was talking like this to me. How can a failure to pick up the phone for 3 days keep you from having your contract renewed for a job you've worked at for years? One you gave up Thursday night dinner with girlfriends for? One you practically gave up kids for—couldn't even have a dog for...?" Her voice trailed off. "My contract was up last month and we were in negotiations for the next one. I have nothing to return to," she says. "Nothing."

I'm a little stunned. I certainly didn't foresee this particular twist. All I can do is offer a hug, but she pulls away. Instead, I pull a relatively fresh handkerchief from my cargo pants, moisten it in my coffee and gently wipe the mud and tears from around her eyes. "May I ask you one question?"

"What...yes...?"

"How did you get mud on your face?"

"I found a clearing in the woods and put my cheek to the earth."

I looked at her, quizzically.

"I guess I thought..." she paused. "I just realized, just now, that I was looking for some kind of comfort—like crawling up into my mum's lap. I guess I was thinking of the earth as the closest thing I have here to my mother."

"You've got good instincts," I tell her. "But I'm very sorry to hear about your job. I know that it's important to you."

Soli looks at me strangely before continuing. "Yes. It was very important to me. So I've been wondering, why do I feel a sense of relief now that it's no longer mine?"

I raise my eyebrows at her, but have no ready answer.

"I was thinking that I might get an answer if I did that—put my ear to ground. That I would hear something."

"Well. That was a very shamanic approach," I tell her. "Did you hear anything helpful?"

Soli grimaces and shakes her head. "Just mud—very quiet mud."

Deepening

To begin with, it is not my job as a shaman to work through purely psychological issues. When there are obviously psychological issues arising, the first thing I do is refer the client to a good Psychotherapist. However, there are times when the soul level work I'm doing with a client necessitates helping them to process trauma.

More often than not, when someone comes to me for shamanic work, they are not in an immediate crisis state. However, the work itself can often bring about a crisis, which means that I need to keep in mind the parameters that I'm working with. The length of the session, where the client is in his or her work, what level of intensity the client will be able to withstand and integrate – all of these elements need to be clearly considered when when doing this work.

When a crisis does come up, it helps for the client to know that the person they are putting their trust in has survived similar turbulence of their own. With most of the people who sit with me in my office I can safely say I've survived at least as much as they have, and managed to heal and transform from those wounds into a healthy and successful person, which makes me a trustworthy guide for the unknown territory they are entering.

A crisis is generally a release of traumatic memories that overwhelms the person's coping mechanisms. Simply put, a coping mechanism is a way in which you deal with pain or fear that allows you to continue to function — to cope. It can be something as simple as emotional withdrawal or using comfort food to cover the bad feelings. If a whole lot of feelings come up at once, they can overwhelm these mechanisms and suddenly it can seem like the world is ending. Especially if the stored trauma includes survival fears, there can be a very intense terror that is difficult to address and control.

One thing that I have to keep in mind is that what the client is going through is survivable. Further, I need to successfully communicate this to them as well. It may sound silly, but it really helps to know that the scary place you find yourself in is something you can and will live through.

Once they know that — despite what it may feel like — this is not a life or death situation, the client can begin to tell the difference between the feelings that are coming up about what is happening in the present and the old stored feelings that are being released in the moment but are really in response to something that happened a long time ago.

As these feelings continue to arise, the client has an opportunity to finally allow the traumatic events to process out of his or her body, mind and spirit and move into the past, where they belong. Much of this is done simply by allowing the client the safe space to experience their feelings and, if necessary, to talk about them.

Chapter 20
The Merry Maidens

The rain is back today, and it makes for a slippery drive through more greenery. We hit the motorway and keep up a good pace, arriving in Penzance in time for a quick lunch and a stop at the local tourist office to buy our own surveyor's map, in the possibly vain hope that we won't get ourselves so lost again. The weather has broken a bit—merely spitting now instead of a drenching downpour.

Soli has been quiet all morning, probably still processing her recent loss of employment, and I have no desire to push her. After a quick meal of cheese pasties in a cafe with low whitewashed beams in the ceiling, we take a short stroll past the pirate museum and hit the road again.

I keep watch for magpies. They pop up suddenly from the tall hedgerows and fly in swooping arcs across our path. Soli is still driving, though I do remember that it is my turn. She hasn't mentioned it yet. We are moving cautiously now along winding, dipping roads through the Cornish countryside. The feel of the land has shifted considerably since before Penzance, and here it seems to change from one ridge to the next.

So much for a break in the weather. The rain is coming down so hard now that Soli has to slow down, and we cannot even see the signs we are rolling past. I feel like we are missing something, and I am just about to ask Soli to pull over and park when she does so on her own. She shifts into neutral and turns off the engine with a sigh.

The only sound now is the steady drumming of the rain along the body of the car, accompanied by the occasional "squeoooch" of the windshield wipers, revealing snapshots of the world beyond our car.

We become mesmerized by this rhythmic view of the world, watching as a lone, drenched cyclist pulls into view over the crest of the hill in front of us and makes his way slowly past us. There is no additional sound as he passes us, so it feels like watching a silent movie from another world.

As if the poor fellow is carrying the clouds over his head, the rain seems to follow him, stopping completely shortly after he disappears. Soli switches off the wipers and we sit, watching the rain bead and run in rivulets from our windows. Soli nudges me with her elbow, and points out her window. I can see now that we have parked beside a sign that reads "Merry Maidens."

The sound of our doors opening brings us into another world again. I smile at the smell of fresh rain and wet earth and the sounds of birds and a distant knocking. Still without speaking, we climb rough stone blocks that offer pedestrian access over a short wall and make our way along a narrow, winding path through rain–drenched gorse and fox glove. By the time we reach the ring of short standing stones, less than 100 yards off the road, we are soaked from the thighs down.

The stones themselves are surrounded by closely cropped, bottle green turf. There are nineteen of them, each standing not quite hip high. Standing at the edge of the circle, I notice two copper pennies and a spray of foxglove alongside the pool of rainwater atop the stone beside me.

Without any prompting from me, Soli enters the circle and turns to the right, brushing her fingertips along the stone as she passes. I turn to the left and do the same, greeting each individual stone in turn. The response is too faint at first for me to be sure, but it feels like they are aware of me as well. By the time Soli and I cross on the far side of the circle, she is dancing between the stones, lifting on her toes and spinning slowly with her arms spread wide.

Something looks—or feels—right about that movement. I try it on myself and smile as I feel the energies of the circle respond and help to lift me and set me turning. Each stone I touch now seems to add to this "lift" I am feeling, so that by the time I complete the circuit and spin into the center with Soli, I am feeling almost weightless. There is no center stone to this circle, so we come together like courtiers dancing a minuet, marking our own center. Looking into Soli's eyes, I know she feels it too, this sensation of dancing with the stones. There is a feeling of joy too, of an ecstatic surge rising through us—and suddenly we are both laughing and the feeling of spinning grows faster.

At once I know that I am "elsewhere"—still spinning and still in a body, but with a powerful, brilliant light all around me. Just as suddenly, my foot spasms and I am back and falling, rolling across wet grass, to stop with the ground still lurching beneath me. Soli is still on her feet, but unsteady. Whatever it is that had us dancing seems to have found its release through us, leaving us dizzy and blurred by its passing.

I come slowly to my feet as the ground steadies and Soli giggles as she reaches down to help me up. There is no need to talk. We both know what we've felt, and it would lessen it to put it into words just yet, so I am grateful to Soli for not trying to explain it.

I stand and look around the circle. There is a gap in the stones to the far side from where we entered, like a gate or a missing dancer. With no idea of why, I feel drawn to exit this way, rather than retracing our steps to the car. With a glance and a smile at Soli, I head off.

There is a wide path of turf extending straight out from the gap in the stones, like a ramp or tongue lapping into the crowding gorse, but it ends abruptly leaving me surrounded by wet undergrowth. I am already soaked though, so I continue on, stepping high over the wet stickery green, searching out firm footing whenever possible. The ground is mostly invisible to me, but I can feel stones turning in mud beneath my feet and it seems to be getting worse. I am almost ready to give it up when a white minivan appears out of no where and passes along the road some 20 feet ahead of me, a road that is completely invisible from where I stand.

By the time I struggle out onto the shoulder of the road, the initial burst of excitement that set me on this little adventure has quite dissipated, and I'm hoping that I'll be able to limp back to where we've parked the car. Turning to walk along the road, I see Soli stepping out of the gorse, equally soaked and exhausted. And there in the clumps of green and yellow, stands a stone disc, about the size of a large dinner plate. I reach out, lift a branch of gorse aside and find a crude figure of a man with arms stretched out to the sides and a circle around his head carved into the stone cross. Soli looks too and then shrugs. But at least I now know why I needed to walk this way. I make a mental note of the image. I can feel its connection to the web of synchronicity. I'm just not sure what it means.

Deepening

There are a variety of spiritual earth sites in the British Isles. In Cornwall, in particular, it's said that 'you can't swing a cat without hitting a standing stone.'

Whatever the intentions of those long dead people who first placed these stones, they certainly provide a link today with the power of the earth, spirit and the realms beyond. You can visit some of these stones and feel the glimmerings of what they might have been used for in generations past. The energies that are gathered there still hum and move in response to your presence and your touch. This is what we discovered with the Hurlers, the Merry Maidens and, to a lesser extent, even with the stones at Montneuf back in Brittany. However, others seem to be no more or less than natural outcroppings of stone. Perhaps these less energized sites were never really 'plugged in,' or maybe we just don't know how to access their mysteries today.

Researchers have found that these stones mark important dates in the solar calendar. In addition, sacred stone sites have alignments with the solar calendar, ley lines etc. There is already plenty written on this and no need for me to go into it in any depth here. A simple internet search will turn up more than enough to answer any questions you may have.

Even with the assistance of professional anthropologists, we cannot know for certain what the people who created these sites used them for. Considering the sacred quality that still suffuses them thousands of years after their creation, it seems safe to say that they were intended as sacred sites. We do know that primitive people in the Middle East and elsewhere placed upright unworked stones to acknowledge the presence of spirit or the divine in a particular place. So perhaps these are nothing more than long standing markers indicating something like 'here there be gods.'

Whatever we can surmise about their origins, it is clear that they were erected for a purpose. The effort expended in moving the stones, even the smaller ones at the sites in Cornwall, must have been immense. It would take much of the resources of a large and stable community to support such a project, so we have some idea of their importance.

We can make some educated guesses about their purposes by exploring the uses the sites can be put to even today. Actually, I suspect that this is what happened with the Celts as well. They were not the ones that set up the stones, but there is ample archeological evidence that they used them for their own ceremonies. I don't know if this usage has been continuous. There are many stories of how priests and ministers have preached against the stones and even tried in some cases to destroy them. Never the less, at every site we visited there was evidence that they are still in use today. At stone sites there are offerings left on or around the stones, while at holy wells there is usually a cloutie tree where people have left their prayers tied in pieces of colored cloth on the spreading limbs.

One of the fascinating things we noticed about the stone sites is that they each have a particular energetic circuit that seems to enable them to be used in a specific manner. For instance, the Hurlers have the three rings that can bring the three worlds into the One Center, while other sites have completely different forms, as you will see in the story still to come. A perfect example of this is the case of stonehenge. I've had several opportunities to conduct ritual among these ancient megaliths, and the sensation is akin to that of a cathedral, while the experience of walking about the merry maidens is much more like entering a parish church.

Obviously, since this book is inspired by my interactions with these sacred sites, they have great meaning to me. So much perhaps, that it is difficult to put it into words. Their impact is both subtle and profound. For me, it has been especially satisfying to work with these stones in ways that might well mirror the intentions of their builders. It gives me a sense of connection with the spiritual ancestors of the work I am doing today.

In addition to the wonderful stone sites, there are also other, perhaps even more mysterious constructions. . . .

Chapter 21
The Boleigh Fogou

I climb into the driver's seat this time, and Soli doesn't argue. Spreading our newly acquired surveyor's map across the wheel, I try to find the Merry Maidens. Finally I spot it, showing us much closer to the coast than I had thought.

"The Boliegh Fogou is around here somewhere," I tell Soli. "I think we must have driven past it in the rain."

"We could have driven past Buckingham Palace in that rain and never seen a thing," Soli counters. "Is there any reason for us to spend more time looking for it?"

As I look up, I see a lone magpie perched atop the hedgerow opposite our car. It seems to be grinning at me. I smile back. "Yes. I don't know just what the reason is yet—but I know there is one."

Somehow I manage to make the U–turn on the narrow road and we are headed back where we came from. Just over the next rise, Soli spots a sign off to the left of the road. It is tucked under the limbs of a rain–laden oak and is no larger than a mailbox, but it reads "Rosemerryn House".

"That's it!" I exclaim, bringing the car into a sudden, skidding turn that just misses clipping the mirror on Soli's side.

The entrance to the drive is a steep, gravel covered drop, followed by a sharp turn. We slow to a crawl, and splosh through deep water–filled ruts and potholes along a dirt drive with branches of hedges squeaking along both sides of the Mercedes and both of us hoping that none of them are the scratching sort.

Finally the trees fall back and we emerge into a open area between three buildings. Two are small cottages, overgrown with flowering shrubs. The third is a larger house, with a long porch and a red door. We park in front and I turn off the engine, breathing a deep sigh of relief.

I am buzzing with excitement as we climb out. Approaching the door of the house, I see a notice displayed there. "Visitors to the Fogou. Please call from town to make appointment to view the Fogou. We have a weekend seminar in progress and cannot show it at this time. Thank you."

I feel cold with anger and disbelief. Soli is reading the notice over my shoulder. "Oh well," She says. "Some things just aren't meant to be."

I quite literally bite my tongue to keep from saying what comes to mind, and I reach out and tap lightly on the door.

Soli tries to grab my hand to keep me from knocking again. "It says—" She begins.

"I know what it says," I hiss. "I also know that I haven't come all this way just to have to turn around."

Soli is about to reply, still pulling at my wrist, when the door gives a sharp shudder and opens. A tall young man with ginger hair, wearing a white apron and wielding a large wooden spoon looks out at us. "Can I help you?"

"I hope were not interrupting the seminar—" I begin. The young man looks confused for a moment, then spots the note on the door. "Ah! No, that was canceled actually. Are you here for the fogou?"

His voice is soft and warm and pleasant, and I feel a part of my soul is welcomed here.

"You'll need to see Jo. He's in his cottage, around back of the house." He smiles and points to the far corner of the house with his spoon. Nodding and smiling, we follow the spoon around the corner, past an old wooden gypsy wagon, painted in every possible shade of green; through an overgrown garden, to a small building that looks more like a shack than a cottage. Jo answers our knock and asks us in. There are just two rooms in the cottage, and it seems more equipped than furnished. Computer, scanner, printer, copier and various other electronic devices take up more room than the couch or chairs.

Jo himself looks like a not—so—distant relative of one of Tolkien's Hobbits. It's not just his bushy sideburns and smiling eyes, or the feeling that his feet really are hairy under the old tennis shoes he wears, but a sense of how connected he is to this place, to this earth.

We soon discover that Jo is the owner of this land, though he describes himself as 'the steward of the fogou.' "This little valley we're in is a Cornish rainforest. It's very alive with nature spirits and the like." He pauses to see if we will be put off by this, but I smile and nod.

"We've noticed," I reply and he returns my smile more deeply now, recognizing us as fellow travelers in the world of spirits.

"I was a bit worried when I read the notice on your front door," I tell him.

"Oh—I just put that there to keep off anyone who's not serious."
He is turning off the computer now and picks up a hat from the
sway backed sofa. "How about a short tour?"

"That would be wonderful! Thanks!"

He starts us off with the house. Walking past the gypsy wagon, he
explains, "they usually burn those when the one who owns it dies,
but the fellow who owned that one was the last of his tribe, so I
picked it up at auction. When the house gets too crowded we sleep
people in it—but it's awfully cramped."

The house is a rambling collection of rooms, with plenty of
windows and beds . It reminds me of the magical houses I used to
read about in children's stories — alive with nooks and crannies
and wardrobe passages to other worlds. I could believe it of this
place. "We've got it set up as a B&B—room for 18—more if we use
the cottage. We have people come do workshops here—on
shamanism, pagan sites, that sort of thing. They stay here in the
house and use the seminar room here for the indoor work..." He
leads us into a large, high ceilinged room, with carpets and stacks
of pillows along the walls and a small shrine covered with stones
and shells and a bronze Ganesh. The room has a faint odor of
incense, overlaying the deeper scents of 'old house.'

We follow Jo through another door and into an enclosed porch,
with a live grape vine climbing the wall and across the glass
ceiling. The room is crowded with overstuffed chairs looking out
over the garden in back of the house.

Leading us outside and onto a path into the dense greenery
beyond the house, I begin to see what Jo means by 'Cornish
rainforest'. We pass under what looks like a rhododendron, but it

can't be, because it is easily thirty feet tall and has a trunk as thick as any tree. Curious, I nod upward to the pink blossoms above us. "Are those—"

"—Rhododendrons." Jo finishes my question with a sly smile. "Yes. And there's nothing special about them either—apart from them being here. The lay of the land rather shelters us here. I suppose that's why it's such a special place."

The path forks through tall, bamboo—like grass. We take the left fork and approach a low stone wall. "This might be part of the old iron age fort that enclosed the fogou at one time," Jo tells us, tapping the wall with his toe as he steps over it. "But I rather doubt it. It feels much too recent to me." My own senses wash over the tumbled stones and I intuitively agree.

Moving on down the path, Jo points to our right where an ancient rowan tree stands about thirty feet away. "The entrance to the fogou is just beyond that tree. We'll stop there on our way back." I look back as we continue walking, watching bits of color waving from the lower limbs of the tree, then we are plunging down a slope into more flowering rhododendrons and the twisting limbs of other trees and the rowan is out of sight for now.

The grounds of Rosemerryn are saturated with life and rain. The trees twist out of the earth, and seem to enact a slow-motion dance in the air above the path. The conversations of many birds fill the air as well, and the scent of the many different flowers deepens as we go. The winding narrow path eventually takes us down to a stream that looks cold even though we don't test it. I'm tempted to take my shoe off and soak my aching foot in the clear, sparkling flow, but not enough to actually do it.

Despite the beauty, all I can think about is the fogou and I am relieved when our tour brings us back up the ridge and we come to a stop beneath the rowan tree. I can see now that the colorful bits are strips of ribbon and cloth hanging from the lowest branches. I look closer and see that there are words written on the cloth and all sorts of other things tied in as well – photos, bells, beads, and even a tiny doll. Jo smiles at my expression. "You've not seen a cloutie tree before then? We leave prayers here, for healing, and – other things."

Jo turns and looks at us, then up at the sky, then to the house. "You'll want to take your own time in the fogou. Why don't you come on back up to the house when you're done?" As an after thought, he adds, "There's standing water in the bottom, so you might want to remove your shoes before you go in." He seems to consider telling us more but then simply nods, turns and walks back toward the house. Both Soli and I peer down into the dark, open mouth of the fogou.

The opening looks like an old mine entrance, with posts and lintel of rough–cut stone instead of timber. I squat down against the tree and begin to unlace my boots. Soli joins me. I leave the boots, with my socks tucked inside, against the tree. Soli nods for me to go first. With a quick prayer to Grandfather to watch my back, I start down the short slope. The hairs on the back of my arms lift as I move under the stone arch, and I pause here, letting my eyes and my breathing get used to this new and deeper space.

I can hear and feel my breath coming back at me from the walls, from the darkness. My bare feet slide slightly on the muddy slope. Carefully I inch forward. Soon I am completely inside the darkness, and my toes touch freezing water. For just a moment, I think about what may or may not be under the surface of this dark water. Then I step forward, gripping my pants legs and lifting them up above my ankles, as my toes go numb, sliding deeper into the cold. My arms and legs and face tingle with the presence of many spirits, as well as the obvious intelligence of the Fogou herself. It feels as if an invisible spotlight is shining on me, revealing me to an equally invisible audience. For the moment, I am mostly concerned with keeping my balance here in the darkness. Reaching out with both arms, I just brush the stone walls to either side of me, but doing so, I drop the cuffs of my pants into the water, soaking them further. "All a part of the experience," I tell myself, keeping my fingers in contact with the walls. On both sides, the stones feel like old bones, piled in an underground crypt.

Now, as my eyes become accustomed to the inky darkness, and I begin to make out the shapes and textures around me, I remember that I am here to do something more than freeze my feet off without falling in. I begin listening, listening with my ears, my heart, and any other part of me that might be able to hear and understand the spirits that I am sure are present in this powerful and mysterious place.

At first there is only the sound of my own heartbeat, my own breath, and a crinkly buzz from somewhere outside. But slowly I begin to move beneath the more obvious, to the not–quite–whisper of spirit voices. There are no words, only a sense of welcome, perhaps a mild curiosity. I move on, one slow, sliding step after another, until I reach the back wall. I can just make out various offerings of pennies and candle stubs; flowers and pebbles; wads of paper and other bits that have been shoved into cracks and crannies between the stones that make up the wall at the end of the passage chamber.

I realize that I should have brought something to leave with the spirits as well. Feeling through the pockets of my wet jeans, I find the shells from the beach in Brittany. Prying several carefully from my pocket, I place them one at a time between the smooth stones. Each one, a separate "thank you" or "hello." I kiss my fingertips and brush them lightly across the stones.

So. Is that it? I realize now that I entered the fogou with a sense of excitement, a sense of impending revelation. But, beyond the obvious presence of spirit here, I have encountered nothing that would seem to justify that feeling. I can feel my shoulders slumping with disappointment and a heaviness in my chest. Such a long journey, to find nothing at its end.

I turn around and begin moving back down the passage, still carefully sliding my feet through the numbing water. Ahead I can make out a darker area along the wall to the right. What is there? I come to the place and reach into it. It is another opening, a small doorway off the main chamber. After a moment of hesitation, I duck my head and crawl in through the narrow opening, and quickly discover that it is a very small—and dark—chamber, just big enough for me to crouch in. Thankfully, the floor is dry and I feel the need to stay here for a bit. My eyes are open to the darkness. I listen again for the voices of the spirits.

I pull my knees up to my chest, squeezing air out of my lungs, wrapping myself tightly into a ball, feeling like a snake under a stone. Slowly, with my breath, I let go of my disappointment. I breathe in the darkness, allowing my eyes to fall shut. There is something more for me here. I know it. But I need to let go of any expectation of what it might be. It must be like a vision quest, where the vision only comes after I've given up on it. After I'm exhausted from trying to make it happen. I need to let go of any sense of how long this is taking. My breathing slows. I can feel my heartbeat cooling, slowing.

There is a sensation like falling through a mirror. I am on my knees on damp earth, surrounded by tall grass, fox glove, and other wild plants. Standing, I see that I am on the upper slopes of a rounded hill. I walk to the top and look down into a wooded valley. I realize that I am carrying a wooden spear with a golden point, and with it I begin to prod the earth. Turning, I slowly trace a wide circle at the top of the hill with the tip of my spear trailing lightly behind me on the earth. As I complete the first circuit, my movement begins to feel more like a dance. Slowly at first, and then faster, I spin myself around the bare hilltop. Beneath my feet I can feel the earth answering my dance with its own song. I feel myself smiling, joyful, filled with an ecstasy that spills out of me in a shower of radiance. As I continue my dance, the ground begins to grind beneath my feet. The resonance moves upward until I can feel the tingling in my fingertips, and through the top of my head. I turn my face upwards to the sky and let the voice of the land spirit sing through me. Though my eyes are closed, I see the hill; the life of the hill, and all the beauty of this dance clearly and fully.

Shapes from beneath the earth begin to move gently toward the surface, like bubbles rising through the ocean. The first one emerges from the ground as I dance above it, revealing the round freckled grey crown of a stone. And then another and another, like teeth budding from waiting gums, the stones rise into their places, still rooted deeply into the earth.

My dance slows to a walk now. My head exploding with joy, my body vibrating with an electrical ecstasy, I move from one stone to the next, welcoming each. The stones respond like the flesh of a woman's nipple beneath my fingers, and there is a similar, familiar thrill. My touch traces the connections from the heart of one stone to the next, all around the circle, forming a great wheel. Having touched each of the now fully risen stones in turn, I move now to the center of the circle and stand still.

Closing my eyes once more, I feel my own heart center, and through that center, the heart of each of the stones. I feel the connections, stone to stone, my heart to each stone and back again. They form a wheel of light, with me at the center, connected to each of the stones by a spoke of golden light. I allow myself to relax into this light, flowing outward through the spokes and on into the stones themselves. Gradually I realize that I too am becoming a stone, sinking my root down into the earth–into the dark, blood–warm soil. I feel a sexual thrill—like electric syrup— rising through me from the earth and from the circle of stones, passing through the spokes to me and swirling here. It is almost too much for me to contain. I feel it on the verge of spilling out and I know that I will need to direct it purposefully. Opening my eyes, I see that one of the stones in the circle has transformed into a slender green woman, her arms reaching out to me. I can feel her readiness to receive this golden explosion. My body convulses as I release the light in a giant spark that leaps from me to her. I feel her take it in and then turn and send it on out into the land surrounding us. That land awakens to her touch and welcomes us. I feel myself rocking slowly into a deeper place.

Suddenly the lighting is different. Grandfather is sitting beside me, and we are looking out from a high rocky perch. He turns to me and smiles. Though he does not speak, I hear his message clearly within me. The deep connection I have found here, with the circles of stone, is one that resonates deep within me, one I need to carry back with me into the present. I want to ask Grandfather how I am to do this, but I already know that the answer will be revealed in the doing. Grandfather nods as if in answer to my unspoken question.

It is pitch dark as I open my eyes and it takes a moment to remember that I am curled up in the side passage of the Boliegh Fogou. I feel the gentle movement of spirit as it pulses and fades. Though I'm not at all sure what this vision "means," I do know that it is why I came here and what I need to bring back with me. I know this as certainly as I know the bones in my body and the earth beneath me. I also know that this first meeting is only a beginning. I thank the spirits and unfold myself from the chamber, emerging back into the dim light of the main passage. As I walk cautiously up the slick dirt slope, I can just make out the faint image of a figure carved into the surface of the stone. It seems to me—in my somewhat altered state—to be a man, holding a serpent in one hand and a spear in the other. Something to think about later.

Soli is waiting for me as I emerge from the Fogou. Silently, she notes the soaked legs of my jeans. Carefully, she rolls up the cuffs of her own jeans. Taking a deep breath, she moves down into the open mouth of the fogou. I lower myself to the ground and slowly pull on my socks and boots, letting the vision of myself as a stone dancer soak into me. I want to remember it, and I'm afraid that if I move too quickly, I will shake it loose before it settles.

Soli seems to take much less time to explore the passage. She comes out quietly and stands on one foot as she dries her other with a woolen sock, then pulls on the sock, the shoe, and suddenly we are ready to move.

I pull myself up and we walk back to the house. Jo meets us at the back door and ushers us into the warm kitchen/dining room, where Stephen—the fellow we met earlier—serves us hot black tea and warm shortbread. I am excited by Jo's connection with the fogou. He seems to have a very deep sense of what or "who" the fogou is. As we sip our tea, Jo tells us the story of how he came to be "steward" of the land here. As interesting as the story is, and knowing that I will be back here, at the moment, I am eager to be on our way again.

Walking out to the car, Soli's feet crunch the gravel drive behind me. "I notice you're not limping anymore." she says.

"No," I reply, looking down at my now painless foot. "It seems I'm not."

Deepening

The vision that came to me in the Boliegh Fogou was somewhat unexpected. I had some warning that things were stirring in my soul, but I can be a bit slow at picking up those hints. And, generally, visions have only come to me after a lot of preparation and seeking.

The definition of "vision" can be somewhat confusing. A shaman might have any number of otherworldly experiences that the ordinary person would consider a "vision." However, what a shaman means by this word is an experience of spiritual intensity which provides valuable and effective information that transforms the self and leads to significant changes in one's life. If the shaman is seeking the vision for a larger community, it would need to provide meaningful information for the whole community that would bring about changes as well.

The practice of seeking a personal vision is quite common for a working shaman, especially when at a crossroads of his or her life. This process, often referred to as a Vision Quest can be a powerful step toward awakening one's potential.

While best known today as a rite of passage for adolescents entering adulthood in some Native American nations, there are many kinds of visions — and many kinds of vision quests.

Most effective vision quests have a few things in common. First, and perhaps most important, is preparation. Before entering into the vision state — the state of consciousness in which the vision may arise — the seeker generally undergoes ritual preparation to remove obstacles to the vision, seek guidance from ancestors or other spirits, cleanse the body and spirit and renew the support of the seeker's community. This preparation may be fasting, prayer, ritual or quiet discussion – whatever works.

In the situation in the narrative, my preparation was the dream with Grandfather and my slowly dawning recognition that there

was an important change coming – which gave me some time to
open to it and welcome it.

The reasons for seeking a vision are many, but they generally come
down to a sense that you need help from beyond the ordinary
world, in order to move forward with your life. You know that the
vision was successful when the information or experience you
receive allows you to move beyond whatever obstacles were
holding you back.

The key elements for an effective vision quest seem to include
need, preparation, support and the willingness to go beyond your
comfort range for an extended time in order to find what you need.

Even when helping my own apprentices to prepare for a vision
quest, the process is a bit different for each—tuned to their specific
needs. I generally choose a natural setting, where the person can be
completely secluded for a specified length of time—often as long
as three days. The preparation is also different from one person to
the next, but generally involves some sort of clearing and purging.
This is often a combination of fasting and a sweat lodge. Along
with the clearing are prayers to the person's ancestors and other
spirit allies for a successful vision. Then the person is taken to the
place where they will be seeking the vision. They are left there
with minimal supplies; perhaps a jug of water and nothing else. I
retreat to a nearby location and continue to support them
energetically throughout the process.

Since my apprentices are part of a larger community of my
students and fellow shamans, even when they are feeling
completely alone during their quest, they are still supported by all
the others. As the vision quest comes to an end, the community

welcomes them back from their solitude with a feast to celebrate their successful return.

Chapter 22
Crossing the Threshold

Soli unfolds the map as I drive us slowly out of the dirt lane leading from Rosemerryn House. The windows are down to let the steamy air out of the car, and the sounds of birds calling all around us in the trees filters in. Listening to the birds, trying to detect separate voices, it occurs to me that I don't know what Soli experienced in the fogou.

"What did you run into in there?" I ask her now. I follow her pointing finger, turning us onto the motorway—remembering to keep left.

Soli is quiet for a minute more, finding our place on the map and tracing it with her fingertip. When she speaks, her voice is tight and she still doesn't look at me. "I don't think it was really important, what I saw."

"...and why is that?" I push a bit further.

"Because you will just try to turn it into something it's not!" Soli responds sharply.

The sounds of the pavement, the birds and a passing car fill the silence for the next several miles. Soli indicates our turns without speaking. I don't know where she's leading us—but I don't intend to ask at this point either.

Soli is the first to break the silence. "I thought we might want to check out the stone circle that Jo mentioned," she says nonchalantly. I nod in agreement. It's apparent that she does not want to talk about whatever she saw, felt or otherwise experienced in the fogou—which of course just makes me more curious. But I know that my curiosity is not a good reason to push her beyond where she is comfortable, so I do my best to be patient out of respect for her process. After all, she needs to move at her own pace—not mine.

I can feel my own vision digesting inside me and I realize that I'm not quite ready to share that with anyone either. I imagine that Soli might be feeling something similar.

Soli's directions take us back into the maze of hedgerows. So far, it's been her at the wheel on these narrowest of roads and I'm amazed at how calm she's been while driving under these conditions. I can already feel my shoulders creeping up around my ears from the tension of not being able to see around the bend.

With this thought in mind, the hood of a farm truck pops suddenly into view around the curve. I brake just in time to keep from swapping paint with the larger vehicle as we both skid to a stop. We are practically nose to nose, with no way for either of us to get around. Looking over my shoulder, I see that a green mini has snuck up behind me, followed by another anonymous car further around the bend. I look to the driver of the truck and he gestures that he cannot back up either.

I lean out the window and wave the cars behind me back. As I wait for them to move, I reflect on how Soli has been managing these winding roads with such confidence. I feel pretty incompetent myself. It seems there's no substitute for experience—either in driving or in digesting visions. Finally the mini reverses around the curve and I am able to back into a wider part of the shoulder. The hedges are poking in through the window and I wish I could pull us in even further, but the big farm truck rumbles past and I let my breath out slowly. I put the car into gear and we move on.

I glance over to Soli. Her arms are crossed tightly over her chest and her eyes are shining with unshed tears. I feel a sense of pressure rising just beneath the surface—perhaps ready to come out now. She is breathing slowly and deliberately, as if trying desperately to control the release of that pressure.

The lane widens ahead as several hedgerows come together in a knot and I decide to take the opportunity to pull over and give us both a break. I park the car on the muddy entrance to a farm gate and turn off the engine. There is a painted wooden sign on a pole with some celtic spirals that says something about a pottery and points back the way we've come. I wouldn't be surprised if these hedgerow lanes aren't the inspiration for the "celtic knotwork" designs. "How about a walk?" I ask Soli. She nods silently and opens her door.

We walk uphill along an even narrower, muddy track between the hedges, this one seems to accommodate farm tractors, horses and pedestrians, but not cars, so we are pretty much on our own. I think I can feel Soli sorting through some internal knots of her own as we walk.

The path takes us past stone farm sheds that look like they were built about the time of the crusades and are still in use. I can see the old farm machinery through the gaps in the rock walls, where the mortar has rotted away.

A small black farm kitten leaps down from the hedge row and scurries away into the weeds. Otherwise, it seems we are the only creatures moving here.

We reach the top of a hill where a clear pedestrian path cuts across our muddy lane, so we climb the turnstile and continue along the ridge. Our path is cut into the turf by the many feet that have walked this way before us, and there is a good feeling up here. The sky is clearer than it has been in days. The breeze is cool but not cold. Everything just feels right somehow. Even Soli seems to be feeling a bit better.

A middle–aged woman, wearing an old overcoat and headscarf, ambles towards us, nodding at us as we move aside to let her past. Beyond her I catch sight of some stones. There are three of them— two standing stones with what looks like a round stone disk in between them. As we draw nearer, I see that the stones are actually smaller than they seemed. The two standing stones only come up to a little above my waist, and the roundish stone—which I can now see also has a circular hole through its center, making it into a half buried doughnut shape—comes only as high as my hip.

Soli stops at the edge of the brilliant green turf surrounding the stones, props her fists on her hips, and frowns at the three rocks. I stop beside her and she mumbles, "it looks like miniature golf for cavemen." It takes a moment, but her frown softens and she snickers at her own joke.

We move to the stones and Soli crouches down and peers through the center stone to the other side. After a moment, she plops down on the ground and rests her chin on her fists. In a low voice she begins, "When I went in it was just cold and dark. I didn't know what to look for and I felt stupid and like I didn't belong. When I got to the back wall, I waited to see if anything would happen. I waited for an awfully long time before I gave up. I was about to go when this..." Soli pauses and blushes a bit as she continues, "...this green woman comes up to me; right through the wall, and pours a handful of something over my head. I could feel it on my scalp. Warm and wet—oily." Soli shudders slightly and stops speaking.

"I take it you came on out shortly after that?" I ask.

"Oh yes! The woman was only 'there' for a moment, just as I was about to leave, and then I was on my way out."

After another quiet minute watching Soli stare off into nothing, I continue, "So what exactly is bothering you about this? What it is you think I'm going to make of it?"

Soli hurumphs and leans back against the rock, looking at me finally. "Well—it's oil, isn't it? And that's what they anoint priests with, right? So I guess you're going to tell me that I was being anointed as something or other. That's what I think—and I don't agree."

"If you don't think that's what happened—then why does it have you so upset?" I ask her.

Soli responds by surging to her feet and stalking off the way we came. She suddenly turns around and glares at me. "I'm really angry with you right now. Before I went on this trip with you, I was content with who I was, I thought I knew who I was—and, oh yes, I had a job! Then you come along and everything goes to shit!" She turns and stalks off a ways again.

I'm not quite sure how to proceed here. I'm used to clients or students who feel this way after our work nudges their souls awake and they find their old life collapsing around their ears. But Soli is neither client nor student. And it doesn't feel very good to have her so angry with me. It stirs my own deeply stored fears that all I'm doing with this shamanistic nonsense is churning up people's stored trauma, in a completely unhelpful way. I start to say something when she cuts me off.

"I know it's not your fault, Kenn. Really I do. It wasn't my mother's fault when she had to wake me up for school either, but I always hated her for it just the same!"

"And you!" she grumbles. "It's like you're a walking human alarm clock." She stalks back the way we came. After a minute and in a bit of mild shock, I rise and follow her back towards the car.

Deepening

Before there were priests and priestesses, there was the shaman, or, the "human alarm clock." The shaman was both man and woman; both young and old; both dead and alive. In order to walk in both worlds, SHe walked in two bodies and spoke more with the spirits than with HIr human family.

The shaman could be called into any human by the spirits. SHe could be called by ancestors who were also shamans. SHe could be called by trauma and sickness. SHe could be called by initiation and by "accident." Once called, SHe could resist, but would have to eventually give in and take on the mantle of shaman. Those who resisted too long found that life was much more difficult when the spirits were unhappy with you. If they refused the call to become a shaman they found that food went bad, accidents happened, they would get sick — and often stayed sick until they agreed to shamanize.

The shaman didn't just speak for the spirits, SHe went calling on them. SHe pounded on their doors and complained about the way they were taking care of HIr people. SHe negotiated the first contracts between spirits and humans; getting us fire, language, better hunting and other means of survival. In return, SHe promised that HIr people would respect the faces of the spirits on the earth; that they would remember the stories of how they were given these first gifts and how they came to walk the earth. Perhaps SHe even set up the first standing stones to acknowledge the presence of the supernatural.

Like so many other contracts, this one is long broken.

For the most part, the faces of the spirits have become ordinary rocks and trees and water. The stories have been forgotten. People generally don't even respect themselves anymore, much less the divine spark that still burns deep inside of them.

And so the shaman reappears. Perhaps SHe is summoned back by the old spirits, angry at the forgetfulness of humans.

Or perhaps it is time to negotiate a new contract with the worlds of spirit—with the faces of the divine.

Nature abhors a vacuum. I believe this applies to human need as well. When we need something badly enough and long enough, we begin to draw it to us, and eventually it arrives.

This is a different world we live in today. The relationship between human and spirit has become much less apparent and important. The role of the shaman has long been broken up in to priest, doctor, judge, storyteller, seer and others. Our connection with the natural world has changed so drastically that most people have no idea of the power it holds in our lives. Instead they believe that it is we who control and direct the natural world. This is yet another indication of how unbalanced and absurd our world view has become – and how desperately we need to regain a real relationship with spirit.

I am not alone in walking this path of a shaman in the modern world. There are many who have been called by whatever it is that wants or needs shamans to reappear. It is up to us to find those faces of spirit in the rocks and stones and rivers — to remember the stories and to renew our relationship with the larger world in which we live. But this process may not look anything like it once did. We live in such a different world that we may not find the faces of spirit in the same places that they were before. In this world we live in today, we need to find and develop relationship with spirit that has meaning to us and to those we serve. We cannot return to a world that no longer exists. We must move forward into the unknown — that too is the role of the shaman.

"Right. So our physical and energetic bodies begin experiencing and mapping the world we are now living in, and a conversation begins between them. This conversation eventually becomes the emotional body. Then a conversation begins between this inner constellation and the outer world, and this becomes the mental body—and of course, the ego."

"So what happens to the soul in all of this?"

"It's still present. It remains the motivating force in all of these conversations. It's the unseen root beneath the tree that is the physical body. It nourishes and supports our presence here. To the extent that it is capable of emerging into the bodies within the world, it awakens and begins its own conversation with everything else."

"I'm not sure my parish priest would agree with your definition of soul." Soli smiles down at me.

Laughing, I stand up and stretch. "I doubt he would agree with a lot of what I believe. But to be fair, I've had a long standing lack of interest in organized religion. For some reason, I have a hard time accepting dogma of any sort."

Soli pokes at me with a stick she's picked up off the grass. "So what is all this about our many bodies if not your own dogma?"

Shrugging, I reply, "It's just a way to answer your question. I don't know how 'true' it is, but it's what occurred to me when you asked."

Soli shakes her head and heads back to the car. I think I may have damaged my credibility with that admission.

Deepening

One of the most powerful, subtle and widely applicable tools of the shaman is what I call the Medicine Body. In essence it is very simply the conscious energy field which surrounds and contains the physical human body. But there is a great deal you can do with this field once you awaken it's potential.

Medicine Body is the first tool I use when working with most clients. I activate it before they come into the office and then extend it around both of us as they sit down.

Many people have a fear that they encounter when they begin to explore altered states of consciousness. It is a fear of loosing their self – of flying off in every direction and not being able to pull themselves back. This use of my Medicine Body provides an energetic cocoon for us to work within. This sense of containment helps the client to feel secure in spite of the depth and intensity of the work while the extension of my awareness into this space allows me to be much more aware of what is going on with the client – on many levels.

It is as if my awareness has dissolved and expanded beyond my physical body, into the air around me. I become kinesthetically aware of the client sitting within the space. The paths of their energy are clear to me. I can see/feel where they are flowing and where they are blocked. If I focus my attention differently, I can see/feel where their feelings have become stuck or their muscles are storing tension. I can detect sickness and imbalance easily, and can respond to it from this same state of consciousness.

The Medicine Body is a completely natural part of the human experience. It is simply a matter of strengthening the Human

Five minutes more, and we are climbing over a taller rock wall, onto a rusted steel plate, wobbling over a gurgling brook. Rounding one more switchback turn, we arrive at the ruins of the baptistery. It is small and the earth has reclaimed it for the most part. The stone walls still reach almost as high as my head, though the roof is long gone, leaving the small enclosure open to the sky.

The space inside is maybe eight by fifteen feet–not exactly a cathedral by any stretch of the imagination. It's more cozy than spectacular, but it also feels like the perfect place for us to let Soli's initiation catch up with her.

In one corner of the chapel, water trickles down the rough wall into a stone sink set into the earth. Along the far end, a wide, low stone altar is covered with drying wild flowers, tiny sea shells, and a bright new penny. This is a place where the locals must still come to pay their respects to the little people, or perhaps where they remember a far older sense of the divine than what they find in church on Sundays. I take a moment to dig the remaining shells from the beach in Brittany out of a small pocket in my rucksack and offer them, with a prayer for Soli's initiation to come—and to treat her gently.

Soli stands in the center of the space, hugging her arms around her and slowly turning, taking it all in. I say "Hello" to the spirits here and then take a seat on the low stone bench along the wall. Pulling one of the water bottles from my rucksack, I take a long drink and then hand it to Soli. She takes the bottle but looks at me suspisciously.

"It's just water," I tell her. "Come on. Sit down and make yourself comfortable. Either it will happen or it won't."

Soli sits down near me on the bench, forcing herself to relax. Leaning back against the wall, she finally takes a drink from the bottle, then passes it back.

"I'm really nervous." She says without looking at me.

"That's okay," I tell her. I close my eyes and move through the doorway at my center and out into my other bodies. I can feel the spirits that live here, and others that have gathered since we arrived. The sense of expectation isn't just in Soli. I acknowledge the gathered spirits and feel around for the door that Soli's soul is calling to. It is here. That seems to be all I need to know right now.

Opening my eyes, I turn to look at Soli and see that she seems to have drifted off. Her eyes are closed and her face has that relaxed, pouty look of someone in deep sleep. Her right hand twitches and then is still again. I'm sure there's a lot more going on for her than I can make out from here, so I turn my attention back to my Shamanic Body, where the view is more interesting.

Time passes differently when in shamanic consciousness, and I am trying my best to stay out of the way and let Soli have her own experience. It seems like it's been at least an hour when I notice that there are tears streaming from Soli's closed eyes and she is smiling broadly. A moment later, her whole body jumps suddenly and her eyes pop wide open, before fluttering closed again. Her breathing changes and I can feel her waking up—coming back.

"Take your time," I tell her softly. "You've been gone for awhile. Breathe yourself in through your center. Bring everything you can remember back with you." Slowly, she seems to come back into her physical body, her eyes drifting open, and slowly growing clearer and more alert. "Now rub your hands together . . . just pay attention to that sensation."

I pass her the bottle again and this time she drains it. Wiping her mouth, she smiles. "That wasn't so bad."

"So tell me!" I demand.

"It was . . . strange. Like a dream – maybe it was a dream. I was still here, but there were all these things I thought were birds sitting along the top of the wall. Then I saw that they had faces like people—and no wings, but they were colorful like birds. I realized I must have fallen asleep and was dreaming. Then I thought about the door and I could feel it behind me. I didn't want to turn around, but I was afraid of what might come through it if I didn't turn, so I did—and there was no door, just this woman standing there. I felt really nervous, because I desperately wanted her to like me—no, love me, approve of me. . . be proud of me—something like that. And I could feel that she really did feel all those things and she opened her arms and I stepped toward her and she hugged me and I never felt so perfectly loved...then after she held me for awhile, she opened her arms and had me look over at one of the strange creatures that had gathered around us. It was all blue and seemed to be shivering, like a little bunny, and all at once I knew who it was. It was Neenah! She was my best friend when I was little, and I thought I had lost her forever." Soli's eyes start streaming tears as she speaks. "So Neenah and I hugged and danced and I promised her that I would never leave her again. Eventually she nudged me back toward the woman and joined the rest of the watchers." At this Soli peers all around the small stone enclosure with a slightly panicked expression. "She's still here, isn't she?"

"Close your eyes." I tell her. "Now just breathe—come into your center. . . ."

"Ah! There you are, Neenah!" Soli smiles and her eyes flash open, staring at the corner of the stone bench. "She's sitting right there," she nods.

"I'm glad to hear you've reconnected with her," I say, smiling back at her. "Was that it then?"

"No, there was one more bit with the woman after that. I asked her who she was," Soli continues. "She took my hand and laid it on her face, and I felt it in my own body—like she was touching my face here. That's when I woke up." Soli turns to me and passes the empty water bottle back to me. "So was that the initiation?"

"Are you still afraid?" I ask.

Soli seems to be searching inside herself before she answers, "No—that's gone. I feel—just happy and big. Like I'm larger than my own skin!" She says, smiling over at Neenah like a gleeful child.

"Sounds like that was it then." We laugh together with the joy that comes from having passed through that doorway and on to the other side. I feel an easing even in my own body as I realize that our journey here has achieved its purpose and is coming to an end.

Deepening

Initiations are beginnings. The beginnings of understanding. The beginnings of exploration. The beginnings of realization. Soli's initiation is only one example of how these experiences can come to you in response to your soul's yearning for awakening.

For the shaman, initiation is the beginning of the larger world. Since most of us don't really want to acknowledge a reality that no one around us sees, there tends to be a bit of resistance. This happens even in tribal cultures. It may be one reason why so many shamanic initiations involve death, dismemberment, life threatening illness and general shredding of everything the person thinks of as normal. In fact, it often includes a cutting away of a person's very sense of identity—in order to make way for a larger sense of self. This is the root of even deeper resistance, as that part of us that thinks of itself as all of us struggles to hold onto the status quo.

It's easy to see when someone has been initiated. They change. How they look at themselves and the world around them shifts. They begin to engage in different patterns of behavior. They draw different experiences to themselves. Their whole relationship with the world and everything in it has shifted.

More often than not, these initiations are naturally occurring events that are brought on by your own internal processes. In the narrative, Soli has a series of experiences which turn up her internal pressure. It seems that for many people there is a part of the soul that wants to wake up, so it organizes a series of experiences to make it happen. Sometimes it seems like this part of your soul is in collusion with the world soul as well, finding opportunities for awakening that you may not be aware of in your more limited self.

Because of our resistance to this process, the internal pressure can become very great, and in some cases, even dangerous. The greater the internal pressure, the more intense and even traumatic the initiation can be.

If you're really lucky—or if that part of you that wants to arrange your initiation is kind—you find someone to help you through the process. As I did for Soli, they can help you to recognize the internal pressure and let it out before it becomes too overwhelming. In some cases, they might even create a ritual specifically to allow that inner pressure to release safely. This allows the process to happen more gently, with a minimum of pain and turmoil. Of course, all the same impact is there. The release of the internal pressure fuels the awakening and transformation of the self–no matter what the setting.

Initiation is a doorway—or rather, as series of doorways—into the larger world, populated by spirits, energies and intelligences that we are not aware of in our ordinary experience of the world. It is an awakening to "what is", and an introduction to levels of our human condition that most people could do without. Which could explain why there are not many shamans these days.

One of the downsides of being an awakening shaman in this culture is that the people around you have no context for your experience. This can lead to feelings of isolation and confusion, as you struggle to make sense of the many new elements in your world. You see into a world that they instinctively know is out there, and which they have chosen not to go looking for. You can see why they might not appreciate your presence in their neat and tidy everyday life, stretching the envelope of their accepted reality.

"It was—wasn't it?" I smile and spread my arms looking around at the terminal, at our lives, at the changes we've both made—and at the fascinating future we are headed into. "And here we are!"

Soli is silent. "But I've come home with no job, no career…What kind of journey leaves you with nothing?"

"If your goal was nothingness, then the answer is 'a good one!'" I laugh. "Sorry…bad zen joke." I clear my throat and begin again, this time more seriously. "But you haven't come back empty handed. You have Neenah, at least…" I remind her, "and you have the makings of a good story, which might be very useful when you start your screenwriting training."

Soli tilts her head and scrunches her nose at me. "They might." We sit in silence for a moment and I search for something with more depth and wisdom, but nothing is emerging. No worries because Soli quickly breaks the silence, as usual. "There's something that gets in my way every time I think about working as a screenwriter. With all that I've learned on this trip—with it all leading me here–" She spreads her arms in mimicry of me. "I'm wondering if I am supposed to become a shaman–like you."

My first instinct, from many years living in the Mid–West, is too soften my words, but I don't think that is necessary here. "That might not be such a good idea. Not like me at least." I tell her.

She looks down and away; suddenly small. I'm beginning to feel a little guilty for being so blunt. "Why not?" she asks, in a voice uncharacteristically vulnerable.

"Well, most of the work I do is as a healer. I sit in my office and work with one person after another for several hours a day. I never know what the work is going to look like, and I don't know if I'll be able to really help anyone on any given day." I take a sip of my coffee before continuing. "As much as you've changed in these past several days, you're still basically the same person. It's just that the real you is emerging more fully. And the real you is still impatient, driven and goal oriented. What would you do if someone came to you with plantar fasciitis, or tennis elbow, and it wasn't healed in 2 to 3 visits? Or, what if you were healing someone of an old trauma and you kept uncovering the same wound, over and over, and, each time you thought the work was done, that you'd finished and could move on to the next 'task,' the same wound would resurface again and again. Could you handle never finishing?"

She thinks for a moment. "No…" She pauses smiling to her self. "I like wrapping things up and moving on." Her smile falters. "Does that mean that I can't be a shaman?"

"No." I tell her. "It just means that you need to be a shaman in your way—not mine. The confusion you feel right now is a good thing," I tell her. "It will continue to shift and change as you continue to grow and change. This place of not knowing is scary— and we don't like being afraid. So, all too often, we rush through it —completely missing the sense of openness and groundlessness that gives us the opportunity to continue forward in a new way, rather than just falling back into the same rut we were in before."

The airport is filling now with other travelers, each on their own journey. The whine of jet engines ebbs and flows as planes take off and land. A smartly dressed woman marches by speaking rapidly into her mobile phone, oblivious to anything around her. Soli watches her pass and shakes her head. "That's not me anymore, is it? But who am I now?"

"That's a great question to keep asking yourself," I tell her. "And the answer will come. Just don't jump into it too quickly. Let yourself keep not–knowing as long as you can. It's good practice."

"But I feel lost," she says. I can feel her struggling with her need for a concrete goal. I don't think it will hurt her to have some direction to wonder in.

"Your gift is telling stories. Maybe that's where your magic lies." Soli folds her arms over her chest and leans back, almost pouting as I continue. "We've talked before how the role of the shaman has been broken up into many parts. I think you are performing one of those roles with your stories. I remember a chat we had back at Mystery School. You said that you have a dream of making films that change people's lives for the better. I think that says it all. What better way for you to use your gifts and fulfill your dream than to write your own screenplays? When you reach someone with your stories, with your words, maybe even heal them, then you are doing the same work as I am — just in a different way."

Soli unwinds a bit as she takes this in. Smiling, she replies, "I suppose you're going to tell me that I should write a screenplay about our magical adventure."

"Perhaps not." I say. "There wasn't much of a plot."

"Of course there was!" She argues. "There was a whole story within a story, with the search for Ys and then following the magpies. There were even some dream sequences. As for action— well, I lost my job—that was enough for me."

"It sounds like you already have it half written," I say, and we laugh. I reach across the small tabletop and peel her hand off her cup and then hold it firmly in mine as I peer into her eyes. "Actually," I tell her with all sincerity. "I think you'll make a wonderful screenwriter–shaman."

She grimaces and draws her hand away. "Just what I needed. The chance to create a whole new career that no one has ever heard of before."

"Not at all!" I tell her. "Just because you know that the work you're doing is shamanic doesn't mean that anyone else needs to know. People will walk out of your films transformed without even knowing what hit them." I check my watch and see that I will need to head for my gate soon. "Trust me. Many of my clients have no idea that I'm a shaman. That doesn't change the quality of the work I do. It just means that we call it something else—something that they can understand and allow to move them."

Soli has a far away look. "I like the idea of people walking out of the theater after one of my films, smiling and open." She looks over at me. "Like I was coming back home from our trip together." She finishes her tea.

"Remember that dream you had on the beach in Brittany? It's a great dream. Perhaps you need to revisit the woman in the dream…the one who gave you the seed. I think you're much closer to getting it to sprout now." I climb off the chair and pick up my carry on.

Soli takes this in and then nods in acceptance. "Perhaps I am, at that." She looks at me ruefully. "Look. I'm not much at saying 'thank you' or 'good–bye', but it seems like it's time for a little of both." She takes my hand and gives it a firm squeeze. "It's hard to put into words how grateful I am—or will be, when I've sorted it all out—but thank you. I hope you got something out of this trip as well."

I smile and nod in reply. Soli hops off her chair, grabs her purse and walks away, glancing over her shoulder and waving once before disappearing into the growing throngs of fellow travelers.

Epilogue

It is my hope that you have taken this journey with Soli and I, and have been changed along the way, as we were. Perhaps your world will now have more room in it for the Mysteries that are the root of our human existence. If this is so, then I am quite happy with the work done here.

The impact of this road trip in 1998 continues to resonate through my life. I have returned repeatedly to the sacred sites of Cornwall, bringing others with me to experience the Boliegh Fogou, until Jo sold the land after his mother's death.

"Soli" has become a successful screenwriter in Germany, where she continues to grow and expand her world in interesting new ways.

I continue to lumber along on my own path of healing, awakening and growth. Much has improved, but I still have quite a lot to do — including the standing stones and other earth based ritual sites that the spirits have asked me to develop. I look forward to these visions coming into focus and manifestation, but I'm in no great hurry. After all, the goal is the journey, and I've reached that far.

Blessings on your journey!

•

Kenn Day is a working Shaman and a nationally recognized lecturer with over 25 years of practical experience in the healing arts. He has served his community as founder of Sheya–a shamanic path of awakening, as co-founder of LumensGate–an annual five day transformational intensive, and as a part of the founding faculty of the SHI Academy of Traditional Chinese Medicine. He maintains an active private practice with his wife, Patricia at Body & Soul in Cincinnati, Ohio and offers a series of shamanic training seminars for those interested in exploring the path of Post-Tribal Shaman. Watch for his latest book on Post-Tribal Shamanism from Moon Books!

For more on Kenn, visit his web site at www.shamanstouch.com.

•

Moon Books invites you to begin or deepen your encounter with Paganism, in all its rich, creative, flourishing forms.